HOW TO CHOOSE AND USE AN EXECUTIVE INFORMATION SYSTEM

HOW TO CHOOSE AND USE AN EXECUTIVE INFORMATION SYSTEM

Paul Rolph
and
Peter Bartram

MERCURY

First published in 1992
by Mercury Books
Gold Arrow Publications Limited,
862 Garratt Lane, London SW17 0NB

Set in Palatino by TecSet Limited, Wallington, Surrey
Printed and bound in Great Britain by
Bookcraft (Bath) Limited, Midsomer Norton, Avon

British Library Cataloguing in Publication Data is available

ISBN 1–85251–176–1

CONTENTS

Introduction   1

1   Information as a Business Force   11

2   What Executives Want   25

3   When you Need an Executive Information System   39

4   How to Choose an Executive Information System   55

5   How to Implement an Executive Information System   79

6   How to Use an Executive Information System   103

7   Learning From Others' Experience   119

8   Looking to the Future   133

Appendix: Common Executive Information Terms   143

References   147

Index   151

INTRODUCTION

'When struck by a thunderbolt it is unnecessary to consult the Book of Dates as to the precise meaning of the omen.'
– Ernest Bramah, *The Wallet of Kai Lung*

The Thunderbolt Factor

Management has been struck by not one but many thunderbolts in the past few years. These include slump, credit crises, regional wars, fluctuating energy costs, government upheavals, vanished markets, new-born markets, tariff wars, labour unrest and global competition. The thunderbolts are raining down like hail stones. Business has been hit by the thunderbolt factor. More information must be collected, organised, analysed, interpreted and understood than ever before. That is an imperative for survival.

A few years ago it seemed as though 'more information' might be the solution to the thunderbolt factor. 'We are living in an information age,' we were told. Now we can see that more information is as much a problem as a solution. Certainly, the solution to many business problems lies in interpreting and understanding information. But, too often, a profound understanding of the problem lies locked in a mass of seemingly unconnected data. Too much information, like the other good things in life, is bad for us. What we really needed, it now turns out, was more knowledge and understanding. Raw information doesn't necessarily provide those. And yet, now there is an answer . . .

1

When water became inadequate to power the industrial revolution, George Stephenson invented steam driven machinery. When the horse was no longer strong enough to move the mass of people and goods that a newly mobile society wanted, the internal combustion engine appeared. Because office work became the new economic dynamic (and corporate overhead) of the twentieth century, men in white coats invented the office computer.

Now that we are overwhelmed with information we have a new tool. The executive information system.

Already stories of the management power of executive information systems are entering business legend. In the US, executive information system-using pioneer Robert Wallace, chief executive of Phillips Petroleum, claimed to have saved his company $100 million using his system. In the UK, British Airways claimed it boosted its share of the cut-throat trans-Atlantic market and saved its stock market flotation from postponement using its system.

Although companies often jealously guard the secrets of executive information systems – increasingly they deliver an important slice of the competitive edge – tales of their benefits are becoming much more common (many will be mentioned in this book). For senior management, the executive information system is quite probably the tool needed to deliver the business benefits of the information age. It is a tool for releasing information locked up in corporate computer systems, for developing more executive understanding of corporate information and of data about the outside world.

It is a tool that can open executive eyes to the role of information technology in business strategies. In short, it can leverage investment both in information technology and in the data stored in computers to deliver competitive edge. It is, arguably, the most important new management tool for a generation.

But, first things first, just what is an executive information system?

What is an Executive Information System?

Trying to define an executive information system presents the same kind of conceptual problems as trying to describe a dog. It –

the dog, that is – has a head, body, four legs and a tail; but that provides you with only the scantiest of ideas of what kind of animal you are talking about. The creature you have described could be a harmless pooch, like a King Charles spaniel, or a ferocious beast, like a slavering rottweiller.

What kind of an animal is an executive information system? At its simplest, it is a combination of computer hardware and software and (possibly) communications. Nonetheless, like the description of the dog, that does little to differentiate it from all other computer systems, for an executive information system is more than the sum of its parts. Moreover, finding an agreed definition of an executive information system is difficult because there is little agreement about what its core task is. An accounting system produces accounts, a word processing system, text. Simple enough. Is it enough, then, to say that an executive information system produces executive information? Hardly, for there is little general agreement about what 'executive information' actually consists of. Anyway, how does it differ from management information, delivered for many years through management information systems?

Should we bother about the definition of an executive information system? Is it just a question of semantics? Not really. If we are to choose and use a new kind of management tool, it is important that we understand what it is and how it differs from other computerised management tools that went before. If we understand what to expect, we will have a better idea of what we should be looking for, how we might use it and the kind of benefits we could expect it to deliver.

Perhaps the best starting point in the search for a definition of executive information system is with the people who first coined the phrase, American management consultants and academics John Rockart and Michael Treacy. They started it all with a paper called 'The CEO goes on line', published in the *Harvard Business Review* in 1982. In that paper, they said that all executive information systems share the following criteria:

'A common core purpose; a common core data; two principal methods of use which are (1) access to the current status and projected trends of the business, and (2) for personalised analyses of the available data; and a support organisation.'

There are four components in that definition which take us a considerable way towards understanding what an executive information system is all about.

A common core purpose. In one sense, all computer systems have a purpose, even though with some the users might not be sure what it is. The purpose of an accounting system is to produce profit and loss statements, of a stock control system to monitor stock movements. However Rockart and Treacy do not mean 'purpose' in that fairly loose sense. The purpose of an executive information system is much more focused on the specific needs of its users. The most successful executive information systems so far have usually had a purpose which is closely linked to the mission and objectives of the business which the system serves. For example, the mission of a business might be to become a global player in its chosen market place. The 'common core purpose' of the executive information system then becomes to support that mission. Different executives will use the executive information system in different ways – the finance director's focus will be different from that of the marketing or production director – but they are all using the system to the same purpose.

A common core data. This follows logically from the first point. If an executive team is striving to achieve its mission and has a common purpose, all members of the team must be using the same information as their route map to the future. Yet the history of business is partly a history of people making faulty decisions on the basis of inaccurate, fragmented or incomplete information. As the size of corporations has grown, especially over the past 20 years, the problems of collecting reliable centralised information about their operations have multiplied, despite the growth in the use of computers. In many cases, the result is that information is collected in different ways in different departments or subsidiaries and there is doubt about what the true facts of any situation are. It is very difficult to reach the kind of shared understanding that an executive team needs in order to strive for its common purpose, if there is no agreement about the facts of the situation. So developing a 'common core data' is an essential part of building an effective executive information system.

Two principal methods of use. The first is 'access to the current status and projected trends of the business'. Despite computers being used in business for more than 30 years, it is surprising, to say the least, that many senior executives still cannot get from them the information they need to understand the position their

4

business is in. One reason is that, until recently, computer systems have concentrated on producing historical information about the business's performance, rather than promoting understanding.

Here is one of the key differences between executive information systems and other computer systems. The executive information system concentrates on promoting understanding rather than producing information for the sake of it. In other words, by 'current status', Rockart and Treacy mean that the executive can actually see what is happening in the business now and what is likely to happen in the future. Moreover, information about the current status of the business includes much more than the traditional financials. It could include other measures, such as customer service, product quality and staff morale, which many managers regard as more important to long-term business success than the month to month tremors on the profit and loss account.

The second of the principal methods of use is 'personalised analyses' of available data. An executive information system needs a common core data, but that does not mean that data will be looked at in the same way by all the executives who use it. For example, the finance director will take a different view of information about staff numbers from the personnel director. One of the problems with other computer systems is that they dump data on a screen or on paper without any thought as to those aspects of the information that will interest the user. As a result, users may fail to see the relevance of the information or, if they do, have to dig around in it to uncover the insights that will help them to manage the business more effectively. The executive system is designed so that information is presented in a way that is specifically relevant to the individual who is going to use it. Therefore the executive information system is as different from any other kind of computer system as an off-the-peg from a Savile Row suit in which even the cloth can be woven to order.

A support organisation. This may seem surprising because 'support' is not normally considered as part of a computer system. The reason it should be part of an executive information system is partly illustrated by another wise remark: 'An executive information system is a process rather than a piece of software.' Essentially, it is an enabling process; – enabling executives to understand more about the business they run so they can effectively contribute to achieving the business's mission and objectives. The support organisation helps the executives to do that, partly through the minimal training that should be needed to use an

executive information system, but mostly through prompt response to requests for future upgrades and enhancements to the
system. So just loading a piece of executive information software
on to a computer does not create an effective system any more
than handing out copies of the score of Beethoven's Fifth Sym-
phony creates a pleasing performance. It is only when the
executive information system is used – as part of the management
process – just as when the music is played, that we recognise the
value.

It is not easy to define an executive information system, partly
because the term has been hijacked by marketing professionals to
cover any piece of software that could have some kind of
management use. Indeed, the term is used to cover PC software
packages, costing a few hundred pounds and mainframe-based
systems, whose price tag can run well into six figures. Some
commentators have suggested that, to overcome these definition
problems, an executive information system can best be defined as
a computer system that is 'used by executives'. However that is,
at best, tautological, and, at worst, rather like describing a Rolls
Royce as a car that is driven by the landed gentry, when it can just
as well be driven by a scrap-metal merchant from Romford or a
little old lady who won the pools.

From the point of view of the user, it is much more useful to
define an executive information system in terms of its purpose.
And its purpose is to help the user achieve their business mission.

Anatomy of an Executive Information System

We have seen that the best way to define an executive information system is by its purpose. Some commentators have tried to
define an executive information system in terms of its component
parts or features. That is rather like trying to define a car as a
collection of named parts. Even so, it is useful to look at the
different parts of a typical executive information system because
understanding the role each of the parts plays in the whole
system helps to promote an understanding of the purpose of the
system as a whole.

It depends on how you analyse it, but it is arguable that there
are seven main components in an executive information system.

Natural and intuitive interface. With few exceptions, executive
and management users dislike computers because they have

normally been difficult to use. There are two aspects to the problem. First, computers have traditionally been accessed from qwerty keyboards and few managers have possessed keyboard skills. Besides, not a few executives find using a keyboard demeaning to their management status. Second, even if they mastered the keyboard they found it difficult to navigate their way around the system, following a path through the screens that lead them to their desired information. Too often, unlocking the screen meant mastering code words so that getting information out of the computer seemed like an act of cryptography.

Executive information systems change that by giving users access by means other than a keyboard and by making the screens intuitive to follow. In most executive information systems, the keyboard is replaced with a touch screen, mouse or infra-red keypad, which looks rather like a television channel changer. Besides that, code words are out and plain English is in. Nothing on any screen should need a second thought or a word of explanation. It should be obvious what it is.

Next, given that all the information the executive wants does not appear on the first screen, the means of navigating through the screens to the desired information has to be simple and obvious, often by pressing an on-screen button that leads to the next screen or back to the previous one. Finally, when the executive wants to change the presentation of the information on the screen – for example, from numbers to a graph – or send a message to another executive, the means of doing all that should be natural and intuitive as well. In short, the system needs to be at least as easy to use as if the executive were thumbing through a paper briefing book or glancing through the *Financial Times*.

Executive database. One of the main benefits of an executive information system is that executives can get reliable information about the operation of the company as a whole more quickly than before. Indeed, in many cases they will not have been able to get that information through a computer at all because their computer lacked a separate executive database. In most large companies, with many departments, information is held in a variety of different databases. Rarely will the information in those databases be held in a way that is suitable for the executive user. Moreover, the executive will often want to review information which is a result of aggregating information from more than one of those databases – and, perhaps, from databases outside the company.

The most technically elegant way of achieving this is to create a separate executive database that serves the executive information system. That also has an important side benefit in that it greatly quickens the speed with which commonly requested information can be displayed on the executive's screen. Creating the executive database leads to another important component of the executive information system.

Data collection and consolidation facilities. Building the executive database means collecting the information from the different sources where it is stored. Rarely is this a simple task such as just adding up the numbers. Often, it first involves sorting out and resolving inconsistencies about ways in which information is held. Perhaps one subsidiary collects its accounts on calendar months, while another adopts the 13×4-weeks period approach. One subsidiary collects its staff head count figures on calendar years, another on financial years. A French subsidiary has one policy on depreciation, a German one has a different policy. Just adding up the numbers and hoping for the best leads to unreliable statistics which cannot be a basis for meaningful decisions.

The executive information system, therefore, requires behind it a data collection and consolidation system, including 'pipelines' into other databases, that not only adds up the numbers but also sorts out the inconsistencies and problems inherent in the numbers. Because that is a huge job in itself, it has sometimes put companies off the idea of an executive information system. It ought not to. Not every reporting system has to be rationalised before an executive information system can deliver at least one useful application; and not all numbers are that difficult to sort out before consolidation. Where there are major problems, the spin-off benefits of resolving the problems in the underlying data often repay the effort invested in the task. Nonetheless, if the executive information system was merely collecting and presenting information already there, it would only be delivering a fraction of its possible value. The next feature adds value to the information presented and the system as a whole.

Presentational techniques. As we have seen, executive information systems are really about promoting understanding rather than just delivering information; and understanding is better promoted by adding value to the ways in which information is presented. Consequently, an executive information system will need ways of adding value to the information it provides, typically by using techniques such as graphs, charts and maps. It will also provide a range of techniques designed to highlight information that needs attention – for example, sales under budget or expenses over budget – and this is achieved by devices such as colour coded variance and exception reporting.

Investigational techniques. Collecting and then presenting information so that it can be better understood solves part of the executive's problem. It can highlight problems or other issues that need attention. Yet frequently those issues cannot be tackled without more information. Sales have fallen below expectation, and the northern region seems to be the worst performer – why? Are any particular branches in the northern region especially at fault? In order to satisfy this need for further information, the executive information system must let the executive 'drill down' through successive levels of data to probe problems and issues. This will be most successful if the executive information system provides data-driven reporting. In data-driven reporting, the screens of information that the executive looks at are filled with information drawn directly from the executive database. It means the executive is not restricted to looking at a few pre-formatted screens which developers have provided.

Planning techniques. Understanding what is happening and finding out the reasons for it do not, in themselves, produce remedies. That is only done by providing the executive with the means to plan and test different courses of action. In order to do this, the executive information system must provide a modelling facility which is at least as natural and intuitive to use as the rest of the system. The modelling facility should allow the executive to game-plan different scenarios and answer what-if? questions. Often the executive will want the results of those game-plans presented graphically to compare visually with the actual position, and to provide information on which to reach a well informed and considered judgement.

Communication techniques. As a general rule, the higher up an organisation executives rise, the less time they spend in desk-centred work and the more time in communicating with other managers, both inside and outside the organisation. If the executive information system is to help them with this, it will need to provide easy-to-use electronic mail features, possibly with pre-formatted common messages ('Can we meet to discuss this?') which an executive can easily send from his or her workstation to others.

Development tools. We have seen that support should be regarded as part of the executive information system, if only because a successful system should be constantly evolving and growing to meet changing business challenges. If this is to be done, the business's technical staff will want to access a range of development tools that will help them build new applications and design new screen formats quickly and easily.

1

INFORMATION AS A
BUSINESS FORCE

'He that will not apply new remedies must expect new evils:
for time is the greatest innovator.'
                    – Francis Bacon, *Essay 'Of Innovations'*

Information as a Business Input

Information will become the most important input for a business
by the twenty-first century. The key challenge of the business of
the future is to manage change – and information will be the key
to managing it successfully.

Yet it is worth remembering that the rise in importance of
information as part of the wealth creating mix is a recent phenomenon. As recently as the early 1960s, economists still spoke of
just three main business inputs, capital, labour and raw materials.
In that respect, economic thinking had changed remarkably little
since Ricardo and other Victorian economists first started to
develop the 'dismal science'. Although Keynes had revolutio-
nised ideas about macroeconomic management, what economists
like to call the 'theory of the firm' remained much the same. In the
sixties, J. K. Galbraith[1] and other economists started to point out
that the model of how the firm worked was changing. The heart
of Galbraith's case was that studying the managers rather than
the owners was the key to understanding how large corporations
operate.

That was important because collecting and using information is
a task for managers rather than owners. Galbraith's incisive
perceptions came just at about the time that commercial data

processing was starting to take hold in major companies. One of the early effects of data processing was to produce much larger amounts of information, mostly about the low level activities of the corporation such as invoicing and stock control, than ever before. Much of this information was effectively unuseable by managers because it was delivered in piles of printout that few had the time or inclination to wade through.

In the intervening two to three decades the role of information as a business input has increased in importance. At the same time, there have been changes in the kind of information used and the way it is used. The business of even a couple of decades ago would rarely have used much other than financial information for management. Partly, this was because financial information was the only readily available and, partly, because the received wisdom dictated that because business was about making money, money was the appropriate measure for management.

Increasingly, that approach to information is seen as quite inadequate to manage a modern business. First, although financial information is important, it is what has become known as a 'downstream' measure of the business – essentially, the product of other, often unmeasured, activities. The financials are what one consultant has called a 'read-out' of the business. In other words, they tell you what happened after it has happened. Now managers have started to recognise that if the problems revealed in financials are to be avoided and the business is to be managed more proactively, it is necessary to follow the river of information up-stream towards its source and collect vital data such as order book activity, average time to deliver, customer complaints and service levels. This information can then be used, together with more traditional financial data, to provide a much better handle to manage the business.

A second business trend that has made the use of new kinds of information much more important is the concept of added value. The concept has been around for decades, if not centuries, but its significance as a management tool has only been really appreciated in the past 20 or so years. For a simple firm of yesteryear it was, perhaps, enough to total the cost of sales and the cost of inputs and subtract the second from the first. The value added was traditionally called the gross profit. The complexity of the modern corporation makes that a quite inadequate measure, partly because many divisions and subsidiaries could contribute

12

their own inputs to the final product. In an economic climate which is becoming more and more competitive, it is important for a company to know where and how much added value is provided to its finished product or service. Moreover finding out about that requires information of unprecedented corporate complexity and detail. Yet as we move into the twenty-first century, it is the company that knows when, where and how it adds value to its products and services that will steal a competitive march on its rivals.

Finally, it is worth noting that information is not just used to manage the production of products and services, but increasingly becomes part of the product or service. It is easy to see how information is part of the product in the case, say, of a newspaper or a consultant researching and delivering a report. Yet it is harder to see where the information content is in, say, a car. Nonetheless the collection and use of information about subjects such as new government regulations on the design and use of cars, new technologies, environmental pressures, consumer preferences and the activities of competitors is becoming a more important part of the value content of new cars. Similar factors apply to many other product areas.

EXAMPLE: US aircraft

In the 1960s, the US F–4 Phantom fighters had almost no software code. In the early l980s, the F-16 had 250,000 lines of software. In the late 1980s the B1 bomber had 1.2 million lines of software. The 1990s advanced tactical fighter will have 6 million lines of software. The software represents part of the information content of these aircraft.

All this means that information has become a definable resource in corporate life. It is a resource that needs to be managed and developed just like any other, such as skilled staff, plant, machinery and working capital. In the US, a growing number of corporations have appointed chief information officers, charged with developing the corporate information resource. In the UK, that task is still recognised only informally in many companies and in others is often given to the charge of the financial director or, in rarer cases, the information technology director. Although that approach may work, there could be a danger in leaving a finance manager in charge of the corporate information resource, given the growing importance of non-financial measures.

Yet whatever arrangements are adopted, corporate information can no longer be allowed to just 'happen'. The whirlwind of global change that has struck the business world makes the effective management of information an imperative.

Forces for Change

The fact is revolution has replaced evolution as the driving force in business life. The signs are all around us. For companies doing business on a global scale, country risk is now a key factor in future strategic and investment decisions. Over the past decade more than half of the world's countries have seen changes that have dramatically altered business opportunities. Examples include the collapse of the Soviet Union, the election of free governments in Eastern Europe, the fragmentation of Yugoslavia, the invasion of Kuwait, the isolation of Iraq, the abandonment of apartheid in South Africa, the dramatic change of governments in other African states including Tanzania and Uganda, the revolutionary overthrow of governments in Argentina and Nicaragua, and the isolation of post-Tiananmen China. The list goes on and on showing that hardly a corner of the world has not been affected by revolutionary change.

Even in so-called stable 'western democracies' there have been waves of tempestuous change that have blown companies and sometimes whole industries off course. Take, for example, the near collapse of the Savings and Loan movement in the US. In fact, there are many different forces for change at work, all presenting new challenges to the business community. Those forces can be grouped in different categories.

Economic. Foremost in this category is the globalisation of world business over the past two decades. This has coincided with the concentration of the world's economic power into three main spheres – Europe, North America and the Pacific Rim. A company that wants to be a world force needs to compete in all of these three markets.

A result of that is that competition in all three of the main market areas has become considerably more intense. In Europe, increased competition has been driven by the establishment and development of the Single European Market (SEM). Industrialists expected the SEM to create increased competition in consumer goods markets such as cars, televisions and refrigerators. A more

14

unexpected result is that it has sharpened competition in service industries as unlikely as funeral directors. Competition has not been restricted to European countries preying on one another; US and Japanese companies have seen the creation of the SEM as an ideal opportunity to penetrate more deeply into a market that had always been fragmented.

Another impact of the globalisation of business is the emergence of an ever-growing fund of predatory capital prepared to wander from one nation to another looking for corporate acquisition opportunities. In plain terms, it means that home-grown companies no longer need to worry only about takeover threats from rivals in the same market-place, but from rivals and companies that they might not even conceive of as predators (such as the new global conglomerate players like corporate raider KKR).

Technological. In practically every market-place the pace of technology is changing more quickly. This has placed unprecedented pressures on many areas of a business. For example, in many companies the research and development (R&D) budget needs to grow as a proportion of turnover. It also needs to be carefully managed and directed in order to serve the long-term corporate mission of its company. Moreover, despite patent laws, the problem of winning even medium-term competitive edge from technological innovation is becoming more difficult. Such is the complexity of new technology that it is often possible to find an answer to a product innovation of a rival within months rather than years. The same is true of service as well as manufacturing industries. In the financial services sector, information technology is used to launch copycat products within weeks of an innovation by a market leader.

Allied to this problem is the question of standards. Technical or market-based standards are now becoming so pervasive that there are few products or services not affected by them. At a strategic level, standards pose all kinds of problems for corporate executives. They must make sure that new products fit in with accepted industry standards – and at the same time seek to mould the industry-wide development of relevant standards to meet the needs of their own corporate mission. They must also find ways to differentiate their products when, in many cases, a growing proportion of their features and technology will be governed by the same standards as rivals.

Social. In prosperous economies in western countries and the Pacific Rim, the rise of the new wealthy has created novel life patterns, based round much more leisure time, and consumers with more discretionary disposable income. At the same time, markets are fracturing into special interest groups such as women, the young, the elderly, ethnic minorities or those individuals concerned with specific points of view such as 'green' or 'gay' issues. In all of these markets, the role of fashion, driven by an ever more pervasive media, helps to shape market awareness and tastes and to change those tastes more quickly than ever before.

Environmental. Of all the issues which have changed the perception of business over the past five years, none is greater than the environmental movement. It has manifested itself in many ways: from the opposition to nuclear power (and, for that matter, fossil fuel produced power); through concern for the destruction of the rain forests; to a new enthusiasm for recycling and products that do not harm the environment. Indeed, the food and household goods industry has taken up the green tag so enthusiastically that there is now talk about new regulations to ensure that it is not used to mislead the consumer. Enthusiasm for green issues has spread far outside the supermarket and station forecourt, where unleaded petrol now accounts for a growing share of fuel sold in Britain and other countries. So-called 'green' and 'ethical' investment trusts and pension funds have found ready takers and, intriguingly, in some cases perform as well or better than other funds.

The management bottom line for most executives on all these and many other changes is that they must now monitor, collect and understand a much greater amount of information than ever before. Of course, they still need to understand a mass of information about the internal activities of their own company; but a complicating factor is associated with this new wave of change. Much of the information needed to understand it comes from outside the company and is often 'soft' – that is hard to quantify or measure – rather than 'hard' information. Getting a grip of this new data flood raises the question of information overload.

The Problem of Information Overload

It used to be so simple. Information about transactions at the bottom of the corporate hierarchy would work its way up through various levels of aggregation to the top. Executives would sit in the boardroom looking at a sheet of paper containing figures, confident that they represented a true and fair picture of the company's position. In the modern corporation, information no longer flows along such simple lines, partly because the old model of the corporation hierarchy as a pyramid is, unlike the Egyptian ones, crumbling away to dust.

The fracturing of the corporate pyramid is only one reason for the new complexity of company information flows. Many managers have already recognised that if they are to manage change successfully then the old hierarchy of the pyramid as a corporate paradigm must change. Indeed, the ability to 'manage change' is seen by a significant proportion of chief executives of already successful companies as a key ingredient of continuing prosperity in the years ahead. In a survey carried out by the Henley Centre for Forecasting,[2] one in three chief executives of 'successful' companies ranked it as the most important attribute for business success in the next five years.

The imperative to manage change is remoulding the structure of major corporations. Instead of all power flowing from the top, decision-making is being delegated to divisions and subsidiaries as never before. Managers further down the old corporate hierarchy are being empowered to take decisions. As a result the corporation starts to look like a cluster of pyramids within a larger pyramid rather than one single hierarchy. Information flows up and down the mini pyramids and between pyramids. So the pattern of information interchange in the modern corporation is much more complicated than in the old. The advantage is flexibility, the disadvantage complexity.

EXAMPLE: IBM

IBM is transforming its management structure from a centralised pyramid to one of autonomous business units. Among the first units formed were businesses to run the personal computer development, printers and storage products operations. IBM aims to make the groups independent, eliminating much of the bureaucracy that hampered product development. IBM is also introducing new management and measurement systems to encourage both independence and accountability in the new enterprises.

As the Henley Centre report points out: 'It is largely the implementation of information technology which is allowing organisations to become more flexible.' It adds: 'The role of information within organisations is becoming crucial in the 1990s and its management a strategic priority.' However it warns: 'It seems inevitable that as the costs of processing power continue to fall and the distribution of information technology within organisations becomes ever greater, the volume of information exchange and the complexity of the exchange patterns within organisations will continue to increase.'

In other words, the price to pay for managing change successfully is information overload. But what exactly is information overload? It is possible to define it as 'being presented with so much information it is impossible to see which is relevant or important'. The effect of information overload is to erect a barrier to understanding. What does the manager who is faced with, say, a two foot mountain of paperwork do? The temptation is almost irresistible to skim it or ignore it. The effect is that too much information – unfocused information, irrelevant information, poorly presented information – is as bad, if not worse, than too little information. With too little information, the manager at least has the excuse that he or she has not been presented with the full facts. With information overload, many valuable hours must be spent searching for the required facts before they can be used. Even worse, having trawled through a mass of data, there may still be a suspicion that other, more relevant, information is missing.

Management consultants have described the problem of information overload in theoretical terms. Most notable, perhaps, is *Megatrends* author John Naisbitt's statement that managers are 'drowning in information but starved of knowledge'. Yet the problem of information overload is brought home most graphically by those senior executives who have actually faced it.

> **EXAMPLE: Minster Insurance**
>
> Esme Howard, chief executive of Minster Insurance, once described the scene at his first executive committee meeting, when he was confronted with a boardroom table groaning under the weight of numerous paper reports. Howard said:
>
> > 'I was suddenly conscious of the enormity of the paperwork we were dealing with. The boardroom table, on that momentous occasion, was awash with reporting documents, mostly numeric, some deposited at the meeting, some circulated beforehand. The sheer physical pres-

> ence was daunting, a nightmare. It seemed to me that
> even if the information, representing something like 20
> different sources, was accurate, there would be very little
> means of verifying the accuracy, nor, certainly, of in-
> terpreting it. The chances of acting on it seemed remote.'
>
> Howard's solution to his information overload problem was to
> install an executive information system.

For the management support professional trying to design a
system to deliver information to senior executives, information
overload is a difficult problem to tackle. For while senior executives generally say they want less and more relevant information,
the solution does not simply lie in reducing the amount of
information available. It is a management myth that executives
don't want to be bothered by detail. Executives love detail. Detail
shows them what is happening in their organisation. Yet they
want only the detail that relates to the problem in their immediate
view. Therefore the detail they want changes from day to day,
hour to hour.

When executives spot a problem, they want to know more
about it, often much more about it; so the problem for the
management support professional revolves around devising a
system that focuses on a limited amount of relevant information
presented in a way that highlights areas which need attention.
That summary information must be supported by access to detail
about areas the executive wants to investigate in depth. In
essence, the problem is one of turning information into
knowledge, but in order to do that successfully it is necessary to
understand more about how executives work.

How Executives Work

The torrent of memoirs from senior executives, like John Harvey-
Jones[3] and Lee Iacocca,[4] published over the past few years has
had at least one useful side effect. It has blown away some of the
misconceptions about the way executives at the most senior levels
operate and has put some of the theories of management academics about how executives are supposed to work into perspective. To begin with, the idea that executives take decisions with
the reasoned objectivity of a forensic scientist, painstakingly

separating out the factors, one from the other, and analysing the impact on one of the other, is exploded for good. To be fair, modern management writers never gave much credence to that idea either. The memoirs show that personal feelings and prejudices, rivalries, jealousy and greed can often play a significant part in taking decisions at the very top of major corporations. In that climate, what price executive information?

Yet while it is well worth remembering that while there are all kinds of pressures on executives which influence their decisions and which have little bearing on the facts of the case, information does have a critical role to play. In fact, hard facts are important at the top and become even more important as a component of a decision with each step down the management hierarchy, as the power to use personal judgement in the decision decreases. Yet this analysis also draws attention to the fact that finding and using information for better executive decisions is not a simple task. At the very tops of major companies, executives use information in an informal and unstructured way to support them in the different roles they play (see checklist 1.1). Some of the information they use comes from within their own company, but much of it comes from the outside world. Some of the information is numeric, some textual, some visual. Some of the information is based on verifiable facts, some on hints and suggestions. Management consultant Robert Reck once asked a senior executive how he ran his company. 'On the basis of gossip, rumour and innuendo,' came the frank reply. So trying to find out what information executives use in which ways is not a straightforward task.

CHECKLIST 1.1: What executives do.

Henry Mintzberg[5] suggested that senior executives perform different roles:

- Figurehead
- Leader
- Liaiser
- Monitor
- Disseminator
- Spokesman

- Entrepreneur
- Disturbance handler
- Resource allocator
- Negotiator

A starting point is to look at the way in which executives work. Here, again, myths abound. If asked, most executives will claim they work in a well ordered, structured way, tackling issues in a logical order and weighing the information in each case before arriving at a decision. It is not like that at all.

John W Slocum and Don Hellriegel in *How Managers' Minds Work*[6] divided managers' tasks into two categories, information gathering and decision making. As information gatherers, Slocum and Hellriegel argue, managers are either 'sensing' (typically, the detail person) or intuitive (the initiator and innovator). As decision makers, managers are either 'feeling' (they adopt a personal approach) or 'thinking' (the logical, scientific approach). Slocum and Hellriegel devised a Boston square (see figure 1.1) on which, they claim, it is possible to map the decision-making profile of a specific manager. Whether this approach is completely realistic is debatable, but it at least drives home the important point that not all managers collect information and take decisions in the same way. This is a point that an executive information system developer needs to have right at the front of their mind.

EXAMPLE: Shadowing an executive

Management consultant June Mulroy once found how difficult it is to define what decisions an executive actually takes when she was working for a major investment bank. The chief executive said he wanted an information system, and she arranged to shadow him – like a fly on the wall – for three days. Even before the full time was up she found he was not actually taking many decisions. Most of his time was taken up with what she called 'comfort meetings', where subordinates reported on the decisions they had taken, and received words of encouragement or warning from their boss.

21

Figure 1.1

Managerial Decision Making Profiles

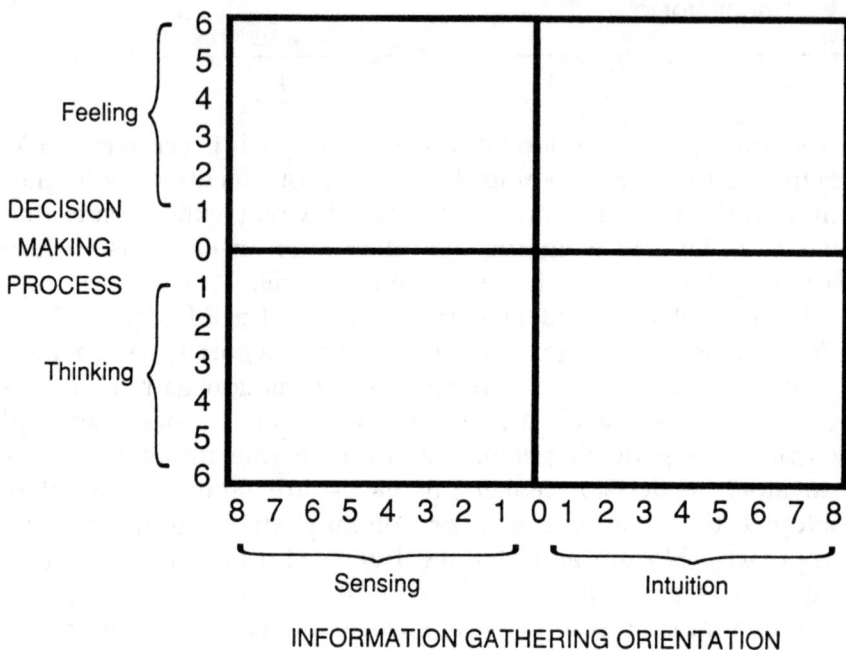

INFORMATION GATHERING ORIENTATION

In fact, when it comes down to it, executives don't spend many hours of a working day taking decisions. Much of their time is spent making sure decisions are implemented – which is why they spend so much time in meetings – and in checking up on the results of earlier decisions. In his paper 'How Senior Managers Think',[7] academic and writer, Daniel Isenberg, had this to say about executive decision making:

'It is hard to pinpoint if or when they [executives] actually make decisions about major business or organisational issues on their own. And, second, they seldom think in ways that one might simplistically view as 'rational', i.e. they rarely systematically formulate goals, assess their worth, evaluate the probabilities of alternative ways of reaching them and choose a path that maximises expected return. Rather managers frequently bypass rigorous, analytical planning altogether, particularly when they face difficult, novel or extremely entangled problems.'

Isenberg suggested that how managers tackle problems depends on how easy they are to solve. If the problem seems to be insoluble it goes to the back of the queue; but if the problem looks as though it can be solved, it gets attention depending on how urgent its solution is. Isenberg concludes: 'Contrary to some management doctrines, this finding suggests that a general concept of what is a possible solution often precedes and guides the process of conceptualising a problem.' The cart before the horse? Not quite, but what executives seem to do is to draw on their experience of solving similar problems in order to find their way towards the solution of the problem in hand. This mental process drives the kind of information they will seek to help solve the problem.

In fact, it seems many executives have what has been called a 'mental model' of how their company works. Effectively, a mental model is the executive's own mind picture of how his or her business operates both internally and in the wider world. The problem for the management support professional is that any suggestion which is widely adrift of that mental model tends to get dismissed out of hand as either irrelevant or as one of Isenberg's 'insoluble' problems.

From a practical standpoint, this means that an executive information system has to tackle problems as the executive actually sees them, rather than as the management support professional or system developer thinks they ought to see them. It also means that the system has to be designed in such a way that the executives can use it in the way that reflects how they work rather than how the system developer thinks they ought to work. In addition it means that the range of information provided through the system must reflect that which is actually relevant to the decisions taken by the executive who uses it.

The practical effect of this is that the most successful executive information systems tend to be heavily tailored not just to the company's needs, but to the needs of each executive who uses the system. In that respect, a successful executive information system should become almost as personal to the user as the family photograph standing on his or her desk. It is this personalisation that is the key to turning information into knowledge. Knowledge can be defined as 'a person's range of information'; and the purpose of an executive information system is to add to the storehouse of knowledge that the executive has about his or her company and its role in its market-places.

2

WHAT EXECUTIVES WANT

'Hoc volo, sic iubeo, sit pro ratione voluntas.'
(The fact that I wish it is reason enough for doing it.)
– Juvenal, Satires

A Change of Culture

Executive information systems could not be successful without
the change of culture which is taking place in companies throu-
ghout the world. At the heart of that culture shift is a new attitude
towards the role of information technology (IT). In company after
company, IT is no longer seen as a kind of support service.
Instead, it has penetrated to the core of the corporate strategy,
being perceived as every bit as vital as the finance, marketing or
production functions. Information technology has come in from
the cold.

Yet it is not too hard to see why it has taken so long to elevate IT
to a significant role in corporate affairs. For many years, senior
executives have looked on computers with a decidedly jaundiced
eye. From the time when the first commercial computer in Britain
chuntered into life – it processed bread and cake orders for the
Lyons' bakery – computers have promised much, but delivered
less. In the heyday of mainframe computers, IT projects frequently ran over budget and failed to deliver the promised
benefits on time or at all. Indeed, for many years corporate data
processing departments, as viewed from the boardroom, seemed

to be living in another world. They talked another language, which no one else in the company understood. Even more important, they seemed to be incapable of learning the language of corporate objectives, budgets and delivery timescales.

Perhaps executives should have expected nothing more. For the early mainframes were pathfinders, seeking out territory never before occupied. Yet the early experiences have coloured non-IT managers' views of the benefits and worth of computing right up to the present day. The advent of the minicomputer and later the PC, which took off after IBM launched into the market in 1981, just complicated the problems. Minis and PCs brought the cost of computing down, but they added a whole new range of problems, such as incompatibility.

As the cost of computing fell, subsidiaries and departments of companies found they could afford the new low-cost PCs out of their own budgets without reference to the central IT department. So they started installing systems like crazy. Many of these departmental systems delivered useful business benefits within their own sphere, but they locked up information that was then difficult for corporate-level management to access.

Another problem was created by the wave of mergers and acquisitions that took place during the 1980s. Companies with completely incompatible computer systems suddenly found themselves working together. The task of developing a coherent business strategy was made more difficult because of inconsistencies in the information that was available from the enlarged businesses or because of the different ways the same types of information – product sales, for example – were reported. The development of sophisticated database management systems meant that it was possible to create substantial applications; but, in the end, top executives found that vital company information was effectively locked up in those databases, difficult or even impossible to get at. IT directors started to hear a new complaint from the executive suite: 'Why are middle managers often so much better informed than we are?'

Executive Information Needs

What you, as an executive, need, is to understand more about your own business and how it operates in the outside world. You need information in order to perform four main tasks – creating

26

business strategies, implementing business plans, monitoring performance and influencing colleagues. It is worth looking at each of those areas in turn to find out what kind of information is needed.

Creating business strategies. As this is the most important activity a business undertakes, it should, by rights, be the area where you have the best quality information at your disposal. In fact, the reverse is usually the case. Business strategies are often devised with either imperfect or very little relevant information. A survey by management consultants KPMG[1] found that 42 per cent of top companies rated their information available to formulate or review strategy as poor or 'average'. (KPMG conducted its survey among 150 companies in the Times 1000.) A frequent complaint was that such information as was available failed to highlight critical issues. The survey found strategic planners 'were less satisfied than their accounting colleagues with the relevance, timeliness and completeness of the information presented'. It concluded: 'This perhaps reflects their more focused understanding of strategy formulation and analysis techniques and the need to obtain a range of internal and external information.'

The KPMG survey hints at the key reason why information for strategy creation is so poor. Much of the information needed for building a strategy is external rather than internal. A corporate strategy is concerned with the company's role and purpose in the outside world, more than with the details of its internal operations. It follows that the business needs to understand the ebb and flow of outside forces that could impact on its future strategy. Yet obtaining usable information for strategy formulation is difficult. Much of it, such as changes in political or social cultures that could impact on business success, is 'soft' information, hard to quantify. Other information, such as likely growth rates in different economies, is often contradictory or confusing. Different economists will make different predictions. Given these kinds of problems, it is not hard to see why you may find information for creating business strategies inadequate.

CHECKLIST 2.1: Benefits of improved strategic control

In their book, *Strategic control: milestones for long term performance*, Michael Goold and John J. Quinn list these benefits of improved strategic control:

- Forces greater clarity and realism in planning
- Encourages higher standards of performance
- Provides more motivation for business unit managers
- Permits more timely intervention by corporate management
- Avoids 'back door' financial control
- Makes decentralisation work better by defining responsibilities more clearly

---

Implementing business plans. Here both the quality and quantity of information available is better, but still far from perfect. Typically, implementing a business plan will involve using a range of external and internal information. The external information needed could include market research data, competitor activity and raw material costs. Internal information could include data such as staff numbers, production figures, costings and much else. The problem here is not so much one of identifying what information you need – much more of a problem in creating strategies – than one of accessing the information in usable form.

Monitoring performance. This is the area where traditionally the best quality and greatest quantity of information is available. Even so, there are still plenty of problems. KPMG's survey of Times 1000 companies found that most companies monitor their performance mainly on internal comparisons – for example, against previous performance or self-determined standards. The problem with this is that previous performance may not have been very good so that even a small improvement looks deceptively better. Another problem is that most companies still use financial measures to monitor their performance. Financial measures have an important role to play in determining corporate performance but, increasingly, they should be seen as just one of a range of measures.

The trouble with financial measures is that they all too often measure historical performance. Even if a company uses computers skilfully to deliver financial management information within a few days of the month-end, the company is still looking at historical information. Moreover, financial measures are usually the product of other activities. In other words the figures on the financial reports show whether other activities, such as sales or production, are successful. They do not measure the factors that make sales, production or whatever else successful. Many executives accept that information to monitor performance is not up to scratch. In the KPMG survey almost half the companies said that information to monitor performance was not good enough in terms of relevance, accuracy, timeliness, completeness, cost-effectiveness and presentation.

EXAMPLE: AIU UK

Managers at the insurance company AIU UK were not only drowning in data, they weren't even looking at it in the same way as their US bosses. The problem got worse after the installation of a new database in 1989. Managers decided that an executive information system could improve high-level reporting. Now the system is used by executives to measure key performance indicators for each insurance line and local branch. The system also provides executives with up-to-date analysis of performance as measured by the US head office. This means that British executives can look at problems both from their own and their head office's perspective. The system lets managers find out the causes of problems by drilling down through successive levels of data, if necessary as far as a poorly performing policy or a transaction which has produced unusual statistics.

Influencing colleagues. This aspect of using information is often overlooked by executives, but it is of growing importance. What makes it more important is the corporate trends towards devolution of decision-making and empowerment of individuals. In this more consensual management climate 'giving orders' is much less significant, persuading others is much more important. In companies seeking to build a team approach to decision-making, there is much more talk about persuading people to 'buy into a decision'. Executives recognise that managers will implement decisions more effectively and with greater enthusiasm if they feel they 'own the decision'. In this climate, persuasion takes on a corporate role of considerable importance.

In your role as a corporate persuader, you need information for two main purposes – report writing and presentation making. Yet in both tasks, you may frequently find it difficult to assemble the detail you need to make a case convincing. As a result, both reports and presentations can rely more on rhetoric rather than fact to support your conclusions. Even if a colleague seems persuaded, he or she might not be completely convinced. In each of these four ways in which you may use information a number of common problems can emerge.

First, you might need to gain more control over what information you can get as well as how and when you obtain it. Too often executives say they feel themselves at the mercy of corporate reporting procedures that follow a company-wide policy but which do not deliver the information they want in a usable format when they want it.

Secondly, you may want to be able to choose the information you review, rather than have it chosen for you. Here the problem arises in two principal ways. Often executives find information presented in a fixed reporting format which may be relevant to some managers but is not right for all. In addition, information is summarised in a way which simply may not be helpful. In fact, summarised information can actually disguise trends that may be important. It can also hide revealing detail. Yet when you see a problem you want as much detail as you need to discover the cause of the problem and then to find a solution. Nonetheless you want to drive the detail you receive.

Thirdly, you certainly want information that is related to your decision-making processes. As we have seen, too often the information you need to make different kinds of decisions – creating strategy, implementing business plans, adjusting those plans in the face of performance – is not available. When it is available, it is presented in a form in which the essentials have to be quarried from a mass of figures before you discover revealing trends and insights.

All this raises a key question. Just what have computers been doing for the past 30 years, if they have not been providing the kind of information managers need? Mostly, they have provided the kind of information that it is possible to provide, irrespective of whether that information is relevant or useful. One reason for that is that many computers were originally installed to perform transaction-based tasks – anything from despatching orders to processing invoices. The management information was considered to be a by-product of those transactions rather than its primary purpose. Moreover, no thought was given to the way in which the information could be used by executives when it was produced, so it was generally churned out in an indigestible format.

Even the creation of 'briefing books', based on the output from sometimes several different computer systems, has not solved the problem. The average corporate briefing book is a work of history, charting what happened in months gone by, rather than what might happen in the future. Except, that is, when the book throws up some interesting facts that bear further investigation. Then it becomes a whodunit with the last page missing. For the briefing book, concentrating on summarised information, does not provide the background detail that will provide insights into the problem. Attempts to get the information will often be met with one of two responses. Either the information is not available, or there is a delay – from a few days to a month or two – to produce it.

Another problem is that when management information is produced in reports it is presented in a carefully structured way. The only problem is that executives don't normally think in a structured way, even if they like to think they do. Instead, they adopt a kind of 'stream of consciousness' approach to thinking about a problem, drawing on their 'mental model' of the business, experience and gut feeling. This means they like to follow intuition, back hunches, explore unlikely scenarios and delve into unexpected places. Unless the way information is presented allows them to do that, it will not be truly successful.

All this might seem to present seemingly insuperable problems for the implementor of an executive information system but, as we shall see in future chapters, they can be overcome. The starting point is to focus on the three key areas where executive information systems can help to solve your real-life management problems.

First, the executive information system should help you obtain a better conceptual understanding of your business. This means that the emphasis in the system should not be on presenting raw data, as tends to be the case in management information systems, but in presenting data in the context of relevant analysis. This means relating one piece of information to another, showing trends and revealing ratios. It means presenting information in ways that help executives find the causes of problems or successes.

Secondly, the system should help you develop improved planning and control for your business. The system really must help you to assemble information from disparate sources when you need to take a decision. Even more, the system needs to help you analyse the information so that you understand it, before you take a decision. On the subject of control, an executive information system needs to improve considerably on current reporting systems by providing ready access to much more up-to-date information immediately. That information, too, needs to be analysed and presented in ways that help you to understand it.

Thirdly, the system should help you perform a number of routine office functions, such as communicating with other executives or arranging meetings. This means that, ultimately, an executive information system will deliver even more value if office system functions can be seamlessly integrated with the information gathering and analysis functions. This is a significant point in encouraging you to see your system as an everyday working tool rather than as a remote system for use only on special occasions.

If an executive information system is to serve you in these three areas, it must measure up to some key standards.

Available. You must be able to get the information you want from the system. If the information is not there, or if the range of information you can access is too limited, the computer terminal will just be wasting space on your desk.

Accessible. You must be able to get into the system whenever you need to. That means you must be able to get on-line to the executive database in the executive information system at any time. As screen shot 2.1 shows, an executive information system is capable of collecting information from many sources, displaying it succinctly on-screen and ranking the information in order of variance.

Easy to learn. You must be able to use the system without too much training. The system must be easy to use. The on-screen prompts and context-sensitive help screens should tell you what to do without recourse to a manual and preferably without much more training than being told how to switch the workstation on. In practice, you will probably benefit from a few hours training in order to get the fullest benefit from the system; but if the developers start talking in terms of days of training, then show them the door.

Relevant. The information you can get from your workstation should be relevant to the jobs you want to do. There is no point in providing access to databases packed with gigabytes of information if none of it is of any use. This may seem an obvious point, but developers sometimes become so engrossed with the technical wizardry of what they are achieving that they forget to ask whether it will be of value to anyone.

	Exception Report		
	% Variance by Countries		
ADVERTISING	1991	APR	Go Back

	ACTUAL	BUDGET	% VARIANCE
UNITED KINGDOM	112,955	89,972	25.54
SWINDON	4,335	1,000	333.50
LIVERPOOL	42,332	10,139	317.51
BRISTOL	71	42	70.80
SHEFFIELD	7,317	5,556	31.69
BRIGHTON	621	0	0.00
LONDON	47,911	50,228	-4.61
MANCHESTER	7,470	8,055	-7.26
CARDIFF	133	583	-77.14
READING	2,625	13,523	-80.59
BIRMINGHAM	139	846	-83.53

2.1   *An executive information system can collect and display information from many sources*

Up to date. One reason for having an executive information system is that it can provide you with more up-to-date information than other means of reporting – certainly, paper-based reporting. It is also worth bearing in mind that up to date is a relative term. Information about staff levels could be out of date in a week, certainly a month. Information about your share price could be out of date in an hour. As screen shot 2.2 shows, an executive information system can update information daily and show important variance data. This helps you to tackle problems before they get out of hand.

Customised. The whole point of having an executive information system in your office is so that it can deliver information to you. It is there to help solve your problems, not those of the person in the next office. You want to look at information your way, certainly differently from executives in other management functions. Therefore you want the way the information is delivered customised to your own requirements. In any system worth its salt, information can be shown in figures, text, maps or charts. As screen shot 2.3 shows, charts can be easily customised to display information in the most convenient way.

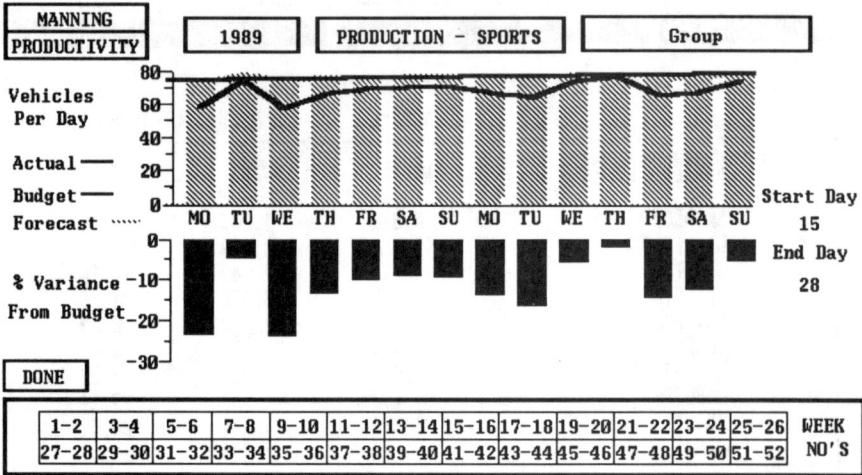

2.2   *An executive information system can update information daily and show important variance data*

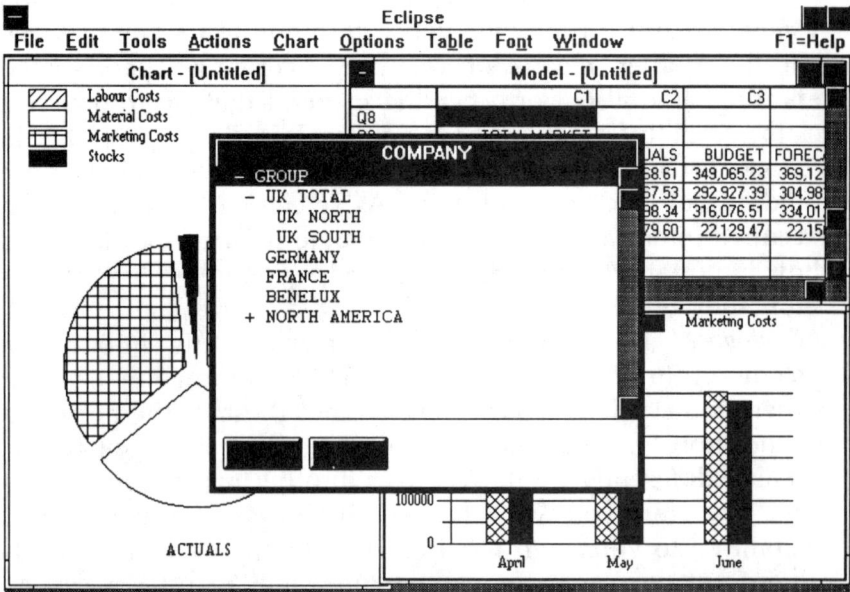

2.3   *Charts can be customised to show information in the most convenient way*

What-if? investigations. You don't just want to review information – although that is an important use for your system – you want to work with the information. This means that you need easy-to-use features in the executive information system to let you ask what-if? questions or game-plan new business scenarios. In that way, the information you get out of the system starts to take on a dynamic, purposeful role in your business planning work.

Ultimately, you want a system that allows you to be the boss and to do things in your own way. That was always a problem with computer systems. They were intended to help, but the sacrifices you needed to make to use them made you wonder whether it was all worthwhile. You ended up changing the way you worked according to the way the computer presented the information. Executive information systems have started to change that for the first time in the history of the information technology industry; but it has been a long, hard haul.

The Rise of Executive Information Systems

The laurels for producing the first executive information system, like those for the invention of television, are hotly fought over. It is pointless being sucked into this debate. Instead it is more useful to examine the different threads which eventually came together to create the circumstances in which executive information systems could be created and used.

The first of these threads is the largely academic thinking which has examined the way in which managers take decisions. This thinking was partly stimulated by the rise of the business schools in the US in the 1950s and 1960s and in Britain and Europe in the 1970s and 1980s. Influential books, such as *The Nature of Managerial Work*, written by Henry Mintzberg in the US and *Understanding Organisations*[2], by Professor Charles Handy, in Britain, focused attention on executive decision-making. Such works paved the way for more specific thinking on how information technology could be harnessed to help executives work. This subject is discussed in books such as *The Information Imperative*[3] by C. Gibson and B. Bund-Jackson, and *Executive Support Systems for Top Management Computer Use*[4] by John Rockart and David De Long.

The importance of books such as these should not be underestimated, for they have provided an intellectual framework in which much of the more practical work about executive information systems has taken place. Many arguments and points of view have been put forward by writers and academic thinkers, but the core of the argument is that the circumstances in which a decision is taken partly, at least, determine the nature of the decision. That argument applies both to individual decisions and team decisions. Thus, an individual stands a better chance of taking the right decision if they can readily access the information they need to take it. Similarly, a team decision will be better if the meeting room in which the team takes the decision helps those present to focus on the key issues and move, step by step, to a logical conclusion.

That thinking, at any rate, is behind the use of corporate 'war rooms' that started to come into use in the late 1960s, mostly at first in the US. At first, these war rooms were fairly crudely equipped with slide and cine-film technology. The emphasis was on presenting, rather more slickly, information that had been prepared before the meeting. Even so, this simple presentation added value to the information over and above that of a paper report, because the information could be presented in graphic ways. Equally important, the presentation techniques focused managers' attention on particular aspects of the information and encouraged them to share ideas and perceptions about it.

Even though only a relatively few companies installed corporate war rooms, they were important because they began to change the way managers thought about how technology of one kind or another could help them make better decisions. A far bigger impact was the introduction in 1981 of the IBM PC. During the 1980s, the population of PCs in managers' offices shot up; yet, it soon became apparent that the amount of really useful executive information that could be extracted from them was strictly limited. Moreover, most senior managers didn't have the keyboard skills necessary to use PCs effectively.

Around the early 1980s, some companies started to think about how the technology made available through the PC could be more effectively harnessed to help executives. In Britain, probably the first company to make any firm progress on this was British Airways, which developed its own infant executive information system as early as 1982. By 1984, the first packaged executive information software started to appear. Today, around 15 companies claim to provide executive information systems software in Europe, while more than 40 purport to provide software in the US.

Yet the systems of today have changed dramatically from the first executive information software of the mid-1980s. Charting those changes helps us to understand the nature of the technology. Computer technology is traditionally described in terms of 'generations' and we can apply the same approach to executive information systems. The first generation of executive information systems were not much more than computerised picture shows. Information was downloaded to your PC, generally from the company's mainframe computer, and you used a graphics package to view the data pictorially. The system probably had a mouse to help you get at the information even if you didn't have keyboard skills.

The second generation of executive information systems, which started to appear in the late 1980s, concentrated on building links between the executive information system and decision support systems. (We will come to the difference between the two shortly.) This meant you could get at the information in the decision support system – itself collected from lower-level transaction-based systems – more easily. This provided access to more information more quickly and also let you develop *ad hoc* analyses of information. You were no longer restricted to the standard presentations in the briefing book. The second generation also allowed you to drill-down into the information to pursue answers to problems that were displayed on the executive information system screen.

We are now beginning to see the emergence of the third generation which replaces what were sometimes cumbersome links between the executive information system and the decision support system with the integration of the two. The practical effect of this will be to make it easier for you to use the information in a whole range of ways, including producing graphs, modelling what-if? scenarios and integrating information from different sources. The third generation is creating a 'co-operative processing' environment in which you can share information with other executives and in which you can use the system in practically every aspect of corporate management.

Before we move on, it is useful to look at the meaning of three terms which we use several times – management information systems, decision support systems and executive information systems. What are each of these and what are the differences between them?

A management information system provides hard data, mostly historic, in fixed formats on regular timescales. Most of the information is numeric and mainly aggregates the results of transactions. The system might, for example, compare information for one time period with an earlier time period.

A decision support system provides hard data, again mostly historic, with facilities for viewing the information in different formats. The system helps to retrieve and use the information in a way that helps you focus on the key issues you need to address.

An executive information system provides both hard and soft data from a wide range of sources, both inside and outside the corporation, to help you focus on past, present and future management concerns. The system works completely intuitively and allows you to investigate problems, follow hunches and model different scenarios.

Having established these terms of reference, it is time to move on to discover when you might need to use an executive information system.

3

WHEN YOU NEED AN EXECUTIVE INFORMATION SYSTEM

'A problem exists only if there is a difference between what
is *actually* happening and what you *desire* to be happening.'
– Kenneth Blanchard and Dr Spencer Johnson,
The One Minute Manager

Confronted by Challenges

When do you need an executive information system? Are there
any special corporate symptoms that point to the need for a
system? The short answer is that an executive information system
can help in most jobs that involve you in reviewing information
and taking decisions.

It is probably more helpful, however, to make two points about
the special qualities of executive information systems. First, they
can help you to meet a challenge. That challenge could be
declining profits, falling market share or the threat of takeover. In
other words, the system can actually help you to solve a specific
problem, unlike some other computer systems.

Secondly, an executive information system can help you facilitate change. We have already seen that many senior executives
regard 'managing change' as one of the biggest management
challenges of the next decade. Executive information systems
help to manage change because they widen your span of control
over the business. By making you less reliant on lower tiers of
management to obtain information, they enable you to view
critical data directly. This gives you personal insight into how
different parts of your business are performing. Apart from that,

executive information systems enable you to collect information from many different sources to help you understand the forces for change both inside and outside the company.

Having said that, an executive information system is not a panacea for solving all management problems. A system is usually introduced most effectively when it starts off with a specific focus. You gain experience using the system for one or two specific tasks, then gradually spread it out to other executives and other tasks. So just what are some of the problems that an executive information system can help you to solve?

1. It can help you to understand the internal dynamics of your business. We have already seen that many senior executives have a kind of 'mental model' of how their business works. Yet as a business grows, the interactions between the different parts of it become more complex. Your mental model needs to evolve in line with the business, otherwise it becomes a barrier rather than an aid to understanding. In any event, while your mental model provides a useful point of reference for making judgements about the overall direction of the business and its broad performance, it is unlikely to help you understand some of the more subtle relationships. Frequently, these relationships are hidden away in the detailed operating results. They cannot be uncovered simply by looking at specific operating results, because the key to their understanding lies in the relationship between one set of results and another – a ratio. With an executive information system, you can build many different kinds of ratios, some of which may give you important new insights into the business.

EXAMPLE: Toshiba UK
Toshiba UK, one of Britain's largest consumer electrical and electronics goods suppliers, found important new insights from a ratio revealed by its executive information system. That ratio involved measuring the relationship between actual monthly sales and the current order book. The ratio – rather than the absolute size of the order book – provided important insights into likely actual sales in future months.

---

2. It can help you to understand your business environment. Unlike most other computer systems, an executive information system can help you to understand more about the economic, social and political climate in which your business operates. The system can help you to access and analyse external information from on-line databases. Of course, you do not necessarily need an executive information system to access on-line databases. Nevertheless the system provides a business impetus for accessing the data (along with the hardware and software means of doing so) and a method of analysing and adding value to the raw data which you choose to view.

One of the most common forms of external data that you can access and analyse in an executive information system is share price. By accessing information about your own and your rivals' share prices, it is possible to see not only how your own company's share price is performing, but how that performance measures up in comparative terms to major competitors, the market in general and specific sectors of the market. Another common form of external information you can access is market share data. Again, you can use the executive information system to cut and slice this data to find how your products perform against rivals in different markets and sub-markets. This can provide revealing information about product marketing strengths and weaknesses.

EXAMPLE: ICI Paints

ICI Paints collects and uses a large range of external data in its executive information system. A news service provides updates about relevant news items taken from newspapers and specialist periodicals. The company obtains a tape of data about macroeconomic trends in its main national markets once a month from the Organisation for Economic Co-operation and Development, based in Paris. This data is fed into the executive information system. Market research surveys provide data about the performance of the company's own products and those of its competitors.

---

3. *It can improve management productivity.* This can be a more difficult problem to identify because the concept of 'management productivity' is, at best, nebulous. One problem is how you measure whether an executive information system (or any other IT investment, for that matter) is boosting management productivity. One solution is offered by IT guru Paul Strassmann in his book *The Business Value of Computers.*[1] He suggests that because IT is used to enhance management processes, the most effective way

to measure the effect of an executive information system on management productivity is by measuring the ratio of management value added to management costs. The executive information system could be used to measure this ratio as a way of justifying its cost, as well as helping to boost management productivity.

On a more prosaic level, an executive information system can boost management productivity by making it easier to obtain and review information that you would otherwise find it hard to acquire. There are really two types of hard-to-get information. The first is information which you must have. No matter how hard it is to locate, you have to find it. The other is information which it is useful, but not essential, to have. With this category, it is tempting not to bother, if you can complete your task without it. Computer author Danny Goodman has summed up this phenomenon neatly:[2]

'Each information level we are forced to transcend in search of a fact lessens the desire to perform the search in an inverse square proportion. If a related fact is two levels away, we're one-fourth as likely to make the effort to track it down; for three levels it's one-ninth as likely.'

> **EXAMPLE: Enterprise Miniere et Chemique**
> French chemicals company Enterprise Miniere et Chemique built an executive information system to boost management productivity on a simple principle: that the strategic information a senior executive might want to access is contained in between 2,000 and 3,000 documents. The EMC system separates all this information into words and numbers. An executive who wants to search for a text document keys in a selection of words that could be found in the document and the system presents a list of possible documents for final selection. When a number is required, he or she works through a hierarchy designed so that the figures needed are usually found within the first two levels from the top of the hierarchy.

4. *It can improve financial reporting.* This is the area most often used for a first executive information system application. Yet you may wonder how an executive information system can improve on the financial reporting already provided through sophisticated financial consolidation and reporting systems. The answer is in

two ways. First, an executive information system can add value to the data you would receive from a financial reporting system, typically by graphing it, comparing different figures, or providing exception and variance reports. Secondly, you can drill-down through the data to find more easily the figures behind the figures. This gives you the opportunity to examine detail when you want to without being overwhelmed with irrelevant figures.

There is another reason why an executive information system can provide a useful stimulus to financial reporting. Large companies with many subsidiaries and divisions often find that accounting information is produced on different bases. Perhaps something as simple as time-reporting is different between one subsidiary and another. Perhaps capital write-downs are treated in different ways. If you have this kind of situation – and it is by no means uncommon – it means you cannot perform reliable group-wide consolidations.

EXAMPLE: Brent Walker Group

The Brent Walker Group's desire to introduce an executive information system was one reason for the group to update its financial reporting and consolidation. The new system consolidates accounts more quickly and in greater detail than the group has had in the past. It also provides a flexible information base to allow managers to restructure the group to meet changing business opportunities.

---

5. *It can improve the quality of decision-making.* This is another benefit of executive information systems that is difficult to quantify, but is no less real for all that. You will almost certainly have taken decisions in the past on the basis of inadequate information. Even though you know the information is inadequate – perhaps it is too old, incomplete, not detailed enough, or poorly analysed – there is not much you can do about it with conventional computer systems. But an executive information system can actually change your perspective of the very same information presented through a conventional computer system or in a paper report. By making it easier for you to get the information, and by adding value to it, the executive information system in a subtle way changes the relationship between you and the information.

43

EXAMPLE: Texas Homecare

The do-it-yourself retailer equipped itself with an executive information system to assist managers in achieving the corporate objective of becoming the largest DIY retailer in Europe. The company needed a system that provided one usable source of information on sales, budgets and variances, by store and product group for the week and year to date. From the system, executives can get information about which businesses are at variance to plan, plus answers to the vital questions why, where and when. Executives also use the system to integrate sales and margin plans for stores and merchandise.

---

6. *It can improve customer service.* Management consultants tell us that customer service is one of the most important factors in determining long-term business success. Yet traditionally it is one of the areas where formal measurements of service levels are weakest. The introduction of an executive information system can provide both a stimulus to introduce customer service measures and a means of collecting and analysing the data.

EXAMPLE: Royal Mail

Senior executives in the Royal Mail, the letters delivery business of the Post Office, use an executive information system to measure the performance of the first-class mail postal district by district. The system provides executives with up-to-date information about a much criticised service. Faced with greater letter delivery competition under the terms of the Government's Citizen's Charter, the system will help the Royal Mail to provide a more competitive service.

---

7. *It can help to change corporate structure.* In a business climate in which managing change is important, it will be important to adapt corporate structures to changing business and market conditions. An executive information system provides a means to help you gain a greater span of control over the business. If information can be delivered direct through a computer screen, you can review performance data about business units that might previously have been collected and filtered up through several layers of management. Direct collection of the information also

provides an opportunity to create a flatter management structure and reduce bureaucracy.

EXAMPLE: Wessex Water

Wessex Water eliminated the whole of its divisional layer of management as the result of introducing an executive information system. The company now operates with a small head office and other staff based close to the operating front line in area depots. The restructuring allowed Wessex Water to redeploy some staff into new revenue earning, rather than paper shuffling, activities.

---

8. It can help to develop strategy. Arguably, this is the most important executive function of all. You can only develop an effective corporate strategy if you have a thorough understanding of the business climate in which you operate. An executive information system is uniquely placed, among computer systems, to collect and analyse external information about the business environment.

EXAMPLE: Powszechny Bank Gospodarczy

This Polish bank, based in Lodz, south-west of Warsaw, acquired an executive information system in order to help it manage change and develop a business strategy. As a newly privatised bank, freed from the constraints of the collapsed Communist regime, the bank is entering uncharted territory. It sees the executive information system as the first step in a new information technology strategy, designed to make it competitive in Poland and internationally. Managers see the system as central to their task of managing competitive pressures in the fast-changing Polish financial services market.

Of course, most executive information system users want a system for a mixture of the reasons given above. A study of 156 companies[3] who had either installed an executive information system or planned to do so produced a range of reasons for wanting a system (see checklist 3.1).

CHECKLIST 3.1: Reasons for installing an executive information system

Areas for improved control that respondents rated as 'important' or 'very important'.

- Strategic planning   84%
- Financial control   82%
- Forecasting   75%
- Market information   68%
- Customer service   65%
- Competitor analysis   65%
- Marketing   60%
- Quality   53%
- Economic information   52%
- Production   48%
- Human resources   39%
- Distribution   34%

Where an Executive Information System Fits Into IT Strategy

An executive information system (IS) should fit seamlessly with your IT strategy. That strategy should be driven by the business priorities of your business. Those two 'motherhood' statements should be obvious to everyone involved in managing and using IT services. Yet one survey after another reveals that IT investment is too often not driven by business needs. For example, a survey by management consultants Develin and Partners,[4] reveals that 33.5 per cent of respondents (517 IT professionals in companies with 50 – 5,000 employees) did not have a business-led IT strategy. Even among larger companies – those with more than 1,000 employees and £100m annual revenue – 19 per cent

46

did not have a business-led IT strategy. Develin's report concludes:

> 'It is remarkable that, despite the persistent and sometimes
> frenzied campaign to lend business direction to the efforts of
> the IS function, lasting now for perhaps a decade, a third of
> companies still do not possess a business-led IS strategy.'

One of the main problems seems to be that not enough end-users
(only 43 per cent in the survey) are asked to spell out the benefits
they expect from IT developments. Nor are managers always
made responsible for delivering the benefits and monitoring the
delivery. Develin says: 'It is clear that many companies are failing
to undertake adequate analysis of their systems development
proposals and subsequently to attempt to ensure the benefits are
captured.' This results in two problems – poor priorities for
system development and a tendency for projects to be over-
engineered. Develin reaches this damning conclusion: 'It is
difficult to avoid the accusation that these findings amount to a
dereliction of duty by management.'

Develin's findings have important implications if you are
starting an executive information system project. If the project is
expected to deliver business benefits – and if it isn't, why are you
starting it? – you had better make sure that the IT strategy as a
whole is driven by business benefits. If it is not, the executive
information systems project will be handicapped from the outset.
It is well worth remembering that, of its very nature, an executive
information systems project has a high profile. It penetrates the
executive suite and possibly the boardroom. The rewards for
success can be great, but the penalty for failure more terrible than
for a screwed-up IT project further down the organisation.

Yet, even companies with a business-led IT strategy can find
that their computers deliver operational benefits but not high-
level executive benefits. The computers perform a valuable task,
but their contribution to the business is not necessarily fully
appreciated in the executive suite. Moreover, as we have seen, a
valuable corporate information resource could be locked up in
those computers, inaccessible to senior executives. You can use
an executive information system to release that information. So
the system not only helps to leverage the corporate information
resource, it brings to senior executive attention the value of the
underlying investment in technology supporting it.

> **EXAMPLE: Aer Rianta**
>
> It is possible to design an executive information system specifically to make senior managers more aware of the value they gain from their information technology investment. Aer Rianta, the Irish airports authority, invested more than £2 million in computers in four years, but senior managers saw little direct pay off. One objective of the company's executive information system was to give the business benefits of that investment much higher visibility among senior executives.

Where does an executive information system project fit into the corporate IT architecture? Traditionally, a business's management and IT hierarchy is portrayed as a pyramid (see figure 3.1). At the base of the pyramid are the clerical and administrative staff delivering goods and services and recording their transactions on terminals and PCs. They may generate simple management information system reports to help them in their work. The next layer up brings in the middle managers whose task is to supervise the layers below and who, therefore, need to consolidate information about the transactional activities in order to take decisions about priorities. This coincides with the decision support level. At the top of the pyramid sit the senior executives whose task is to decide strategy, make policy and set objectives. To do this, they must review information about the operation of the business and make judgements about it. This corresponds to the executive information system level.

Of course, this is a simplified view of a corporate hierarchy but may have accurately represented what happened in years gone by. Today, it is increasingly misleading to think in those terms. Some management thinkers have attempted to represent the corporate organisation in simple diagrammatic terms. One of the most noteworthy is Noel Austin whose paper 'A management support environment'[5] suggested that the company should be viewed as two pyramids, one standing on its base representing the organisation, the other standing on its apex and superimposed over the first representing the company information needs.

In fact, the modern company's information needs are probably best represented not by one but a series of pyramids (see figure 3.2). Modern management theories about decentralisation and empowerment have created a situation in which a large company tends to have a central head office and a number of divisions and

Figure 3.1

Traditional Information Hierarchy

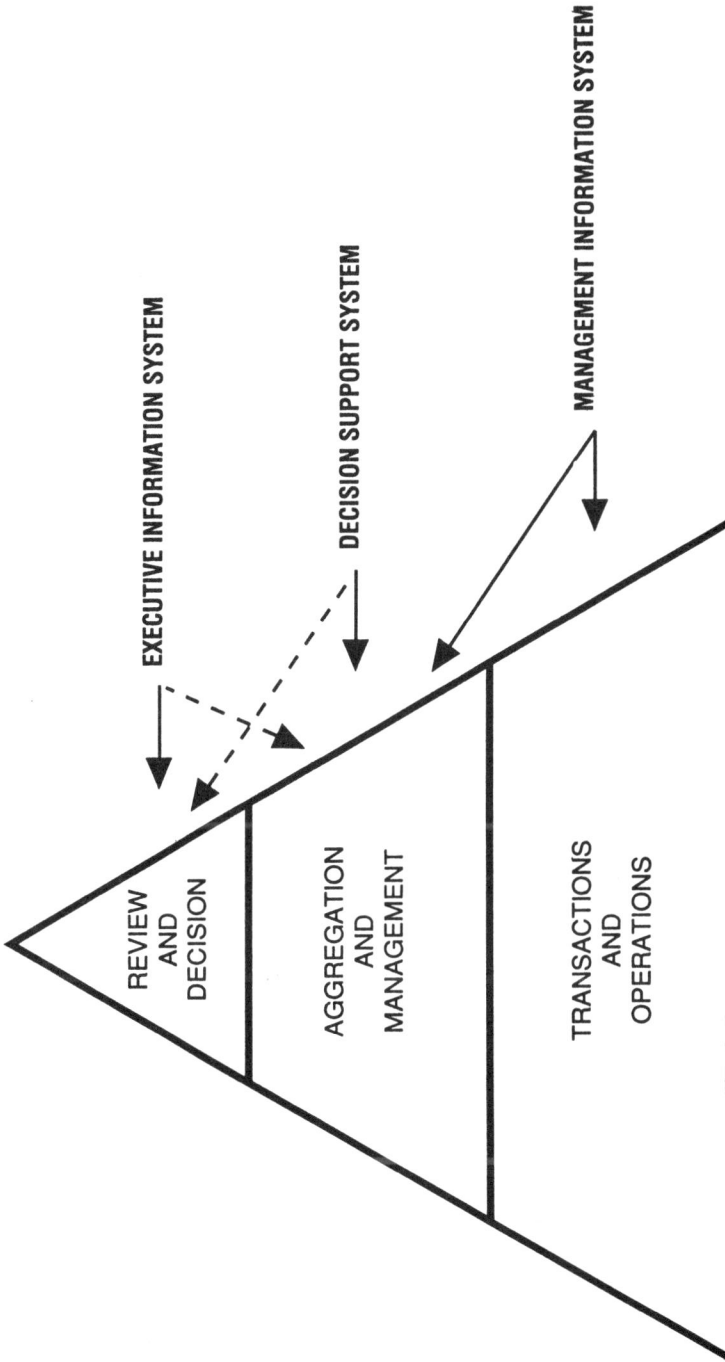

EXECUTIVE INFORMATION SYSTEM

DECISION SUPPORT SYSTEM

MANAGEMENT INFORMATION SYSTEM

REVIEW AND DECISION

AGGREGATION AND MANAGEMENT

TRANSACTIONS AND OPERATIONS

Figure 3.2

New Information Hierarchy

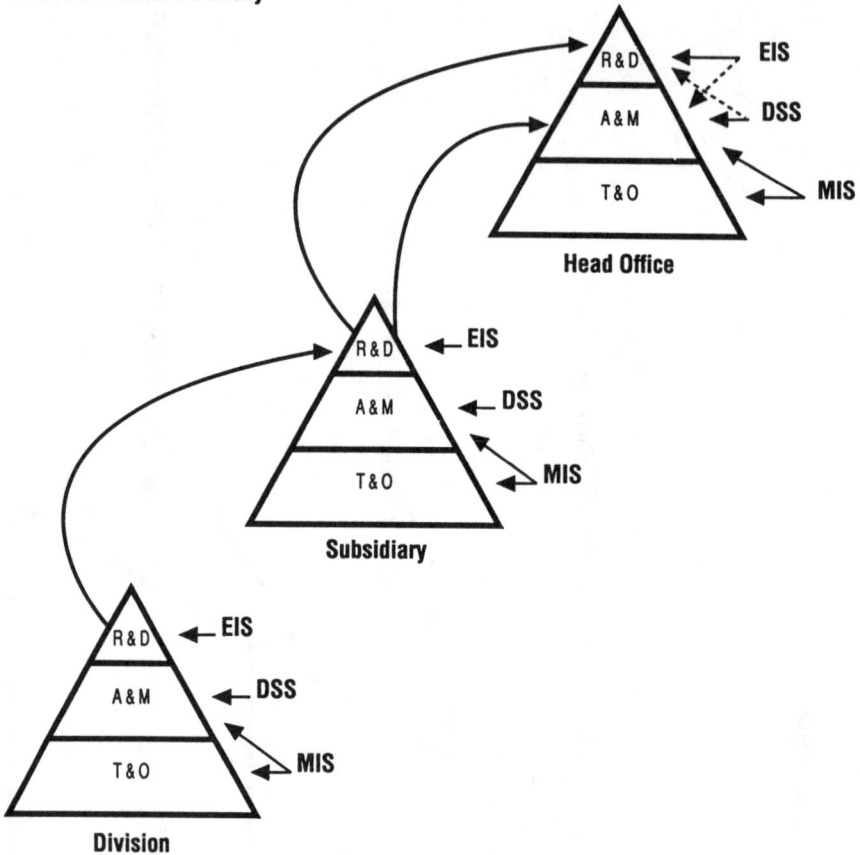

subsidiaries. These divisions are all management pyramids in their own right with the transaction, consolidation and analysis levels. What then happens is that the head office collects the results of the divisions' consolidations and analyses in order to perform its own reviews. It may also collect information from external data providers, which could be looked at as additional pyramids in the cluster.

The arrangement of the cluster of pyramids will, of course, be different in detail from one company to another. Nonetheless it is important that you should have a clear picture of what it is before you embark on an executive information system project. That picture will give you a view of where information resides in your organisation, and what steps will have to be taken to capture it in the system.

Who Should use an Executive Information System?

An executive is the obvious answer to the question. But just what is an executive? And how does he or she differ, if at all, from a manager? There can be no precise boundaries to the definitions of 'executive' and 'manager'. One way to look at the difference is as the executive in the role of policy maker and the manager in the role of policy implementor. This definition can be quite helpful when considering the specific features of an executive information system, because the system needs to provide the special mix of information that policy makers need. As we have already seen, that mix includes soft as well as hard information and external as well as internal data.

In practice, most users of executive information systems to date have been in the top two or three tiers of management within an operating unit. What those layers represent depends on the size and structure of the company, but in a large company – say Times 500 size – it would include board-level directors, executive committee members, other departmental heads or their deputies. In addition, executive information systems are also used by business analysts whose task is to collect and analyse information for these senior executives. While many executive information systems are installed in head offices, others are installed in divisions or subsidiaries. Where this is the case, the users generally mirror the same level as head office users. The divisional or subsidiary executive information system is becoming much more common and will continue to do so in the years ahead.

There are two schools of thought about who should have the opportunity to use an executive information system. One group thinks the executive information system provides such sensitive and strategically important information it should be restricted to senior group managers.

The other group believes that executive information systems are too good to be restricted just to top executives. That is the view that seems to be gaining ground. Executive information systems are spreading through the organisation. Whereas typical executive information systems might have had just half a dozen or ten users a couple of years ago, now figures of 20 or more users are by no means unusual.

Although executive information system use is spreading among a wide range of different executives, it is worth picking out three groups for special comment.

Chief executives and managing directors. Traditionally, this group has resisted using computers but is now often the most enthusiastic champion of executive information system projects. The combination of easy information access and analysis features has handed managing directors a tool that lets them view their company's business performance in the context of its total market-place. It has also freed them from the necessity to obtain information from other executives or business managers. Several have said that this direct access to the fountain head of information has helped to free them from a 'corporate view' and take a fresh look at the facts of the situation.

EXAMPLE: Rank Xerox

Rank Xerox is building a fine tradition of managing directors using an executive information system. Both the present and previous MDs have used the system in their task of tackling the major challenges to Rank Xerox's core business. Along with about 40 other executives, the MD can access Rank Xerox's system for information about strategic issues such as business outlook and activity data, sales figures and manpower planning. The system is linked with electronic mail so that the MD can make notes on specific screens of information, key in messages and file them for future use or send to other executives.

Finance directors, financial controllers and other senior finance executives. These have often used computers in the past but been frustrated by their inability to get information analysed in just the way they want it without being overwhelmed with detail. The executive information system provides the best reporting and analysis tool for financial data they have ever had, plus the chance to get information from other non-financial sources.

EXAMPLE: Co-operative Wholesale Society

Alan Prescott, financial controller for the Co-operative Whole-sale Society, uses an executive information system to monitor key performance indicators including use of working capital, cash-flow and profit in different trading divisions. The system lets Prescott interpret information that was impossible using the former accounting schedules. He gains new insights into the information through the use of graphs and colour-coded exception reports.

Marketing and sales executives. Some executive information systems are used in vertical applications; probably so far the most common area. The marketing and sales directors' problem is similar to that faced by financial executives – the need to review large amounts of information. By focusing similar analysis tools on marketing and sales data, these managers can gain new insights into their aspect of the business.

EXAMPLE: Gateway Foodmarkets

Gateway is one of Britain's major supermarket chains with more than 700 stores. Because of the wide variation in the size of the stores and their catchment areas, managers need to take complex decisions about the product mix in each store. The company's executive information system helps managers determine the customer profile of each store catchment area and then match the merchandise offered to meet that customer profile. The system has helped managers to introduce more effective merchandising procedures and reduce the number of decision points. Managers reckon the system has directly aided profit improvement.

At the moment, executive information systems are mostly used by individuals in their own offices, either alone or in small groups. But, increasingly, the systems are used for group decision making in the board or executive committee. This is important for it enables a company's most senior executives to review one set of information – the same version of the 'corporate truth' – and gain shared insights from the information.

However the system is used, it is important to think through the policy issues that might be raised in your company even

even before you embark on an executive information system project. Some of the issues you should address are listed in checklist 3.2.

CHECKLIST 3.2: Issues to consider at the start of a project

- What are the objectives of the system?
- What is the scope of the first phase?
- What about future phases?
- Who will sponsor the project?
- Who will develop the project?
- Who will specify requirements?
- Who will sign off requirements?
- Which executives will be users in phase one?
- And which in future phases?
- Will the system be restricted to executives?
- Who will own the system?

4

HOW TO CHOOSE AN EXECUTIVE INFORMATION SYSTEM

'We are more easily persuaded, in general, by the reasons we ourselves discover than by those which are given to us by others.'

– Blaise Pascal, Pensées

Why Executive Information System Choice is a Business Issue

Choosing an executive information system is a business not a technical issue. Unless you get that central point firmly embedded in your mind, your project is almost certainly doomed to fail. As we have seen in the last chapter, an executive information system project, like any other project involving the use of information technology, needs to be driven by business needs. However that is not enough. Because an executive information system is a business rather than an IT project, it cannot be managed like one.

Who initiates an executive information system project? Researchers at the Oxford Institute of Information Management asked 36 companies using an executive information system who had the idea. In five cases it was the chief executive or managing director, in 12 cases a director and in 14 cases a manager (five didn't say). In 13 cases, the idea originated in the IT department, in eight in finance, in three in business planning and in three in other departments (nine of the respondents didn't say).

Why is an executive information system so different from other computer projects? The central point is that an executive information system is not about technology but about management processes. The reasons for wanting an executive information system are connected with changing the way executives work, for example in changing the way they carry out their planning and control functions. This means that your executive information systems project will have a deep impact upon the way in which the executives who use the system will do their work in the future. Issues affected include their span of control (the effective reach they can make over the business), working practices (especially how they collect and use information), and their decision taking (especially how they use information in conjunction with other executives to formulate new corporate policies).

Those important differences alone would warrant you taking a different approach to an executive information system. In fact, the introduction of such a system will have an impact beyond those senior executives lucky enough to use it. Like an earthquake, the tremors from the executive information system will ripple out, even to the furthest extremities of the organisation. Unlike the earthquake, the effects will be constructive (providing you introduce the executive information system thoughtfully and sympathetically) but they might be seen as destructive by managers in other parts of the organisation. Managers who might be especially hostile are those who have traditionally provided information direct to senior executives and who see the new system as an unwelcome interloper cutting off their contact with the apex of the organisation. Other potential executive information system enemies are managers who see their role threatened because the system removes part of their work function, for example, in collecting and analysing information or preparing reports. So you will need to deal with these 'political' and 'social' issues when you come to implement the executive information system.

But the fallout from the executive information system will not be limited to other managers. There will be an impact on your company's information systems strategy. Quite simply, implementing an executive information system project, with a high visibility to the most senior managers, will expose deficiencies in the existing information systems which they will probably want to remedy. They might be minor, such as small inconsistencies in the ways standard information is collected from different parts of the organisation. They might be major, such as the lack of a forward strategy for integrating different and incompatible computer systems to facilitate the easier exchange and mutual use of corporate information.

The checklist below looks at some of the people you may encounter in an executive information system project, the problems they may cause and the ways of tackling them.

CHECKLIST 4.1: People who can cause trouble for an executive information system project

- Managers reporting directly to the executive information system user.
  Cause: they see the system threatening their rapport with the top dog.
  Remedy: involve them in the project.
- IT staff.
  Cause: the project seems to transgress on to their hallowed turf.
  Remedy: include someone from IT department on the project team.
- Managers who will provide data for the system.
  Cause: the top dog will get direct access to 'their' data. Inadequacies in it, which until now they have effectively disguised, will be exposed.
  Remedy: make them retain 'ownership' of the data. Provide them with resources to clean up dirty data.
- Potential users of the system.
  Cause: worry about looking a fool trying to use a computer.
  Remedy: make the system easy and intuitive to use. Tailor it to their specific needs. Conduct one-to-one training.

So when you embark on an executive information system, you open a box from which many surprises, both pleasant and unpleasant, can emerge. That is why it is so important to have thought through the project strategy before detailed work begins. Several hundred companies in Britain, and many more overseas, have already implemented executive information systems projects. From those systems, a wealth of experience has emerged which you can draw on as you start your own project.

Right at the outset, you need to understand that your project stands a much higher chance of success if it is backed by an enthusiastic champion and/or sponsor. The role of the champion and sponsor is so important it is dealt with in a separate section below. Other issues you need to address include these:

Identify the key business issue(s) to be addressed by the system. You need to do this in conjunction with the champion and sponsor together with, ideally, any other users of the system. If you are introducing an executive information system for the first time, it pays to start off with relatively modest aims. No doubt there is a myriad of issues in your company that could be tackled. Don't be mesmerised by them all. Instead, focus on one pressing issue where (a) a system will deliver real and demonstrable benefits and (b) you can achieve quick results. The first point is important because you only generally get one chance to introduce an executive information system. If you louse it up, the executive users write it – and sometimes you – off. The second point is important because senior executives are notoriously impatient. They are used to demanding and getting things done 'yesterday' and they have little concept of development timescales in information technology projects.

Manage the politics of the project. Even a small project will have a political dimension. There will be managers whose noses will be disjointed. Others who have a vested interest in making it fail. The worst thing to do is to pretend these problems don't exist. Even though they are difficult, and require people management rather than technical skills to solve, they need to be tackled right at the outset of the project.

Put together a project team with the right mix of skills. Apart from the champion or sponsor, you will need somebody from the IT department to provide the needed technical nous. You will also need to involve a manager with detailed knowledge of the chosen application and someone to represent the 'data providers', those managers who will provide the information that will ultimately be used in the executive information system. Persuading managers such as these to 'buy into' the project right at the outset helps to reduce some of the resistance you will encounter on the way.

A useful kind of person to have involved on your project team is a 'hybrid manager'. These were first identified in a British Computer Society (BCS) report[1] that called for more managers combining business and technological skills. According to the BCS, the desired characteristics of these paragons are:

1. Technological competence: they have a knowledge base that allows them to recognise an IT opportunity, scale its size and

complexity, know what needs to be done and perhaps prototype it.

2. Business confidence: they have the experience and knowledge of the business area in which they work, so that they can recognise an application opportunity, make the case for it, see how it fits into existing business operations and systems, and anticipate the implementation issues.

3. Organisational skills: they know whom to call for support in the IT function, who should be enlisted in the user area, and when and how is the right time to initiate an idea. They also have the social and political skills to make things happen and survive the ambiguities of their role.

The BCS description of a hybrid manager is an almost perfect job description for an executive information system project leader.

Ensure you can get the data to make the application work. This is such a central issue it needs to be closely examined when drawing up the project strategy and not handed over to the technical people to sort out as a kind of afterthought. At the end of the day, the application will only work if you can get the right information into it. That may not be possible and it is unlikely to be easy. Apart from the issue of resistance to handing over the informa-tion – managers like to think they 'own' their data and, as we shall see, that is a useful concept to foster – there may be technical problems in collecting the data and downloading it into the executive information systems. The checklist below provides you with some of the questions you need to ask when examining the data issues.

CHECKLIST 4.2: Questions to ask about data

- Does it exist?
- If it does, does it exist in the right format?
- If it doesn't, can it be massaged into the right format?
- What inconsistencies in it will need to be ironed out?
- Is it collected in the time periods, reporting units, etc. needed for the executive information system?
- Can it be accessed across the communication links and with the software that will be used in the project?

Be honest about what the first project can achieve. IT professionals have too often damaged their cause in the past by promising too much. Sometimes they have done so in order to win the executive go-ahead for a project. As most non-technical managers know, however, the history of IT investment is a history of too many promises and not enough performance. (This could be a good reason for distancing the central responsibility for the project from the IT department.) You need to walk a careful line in presenting the project to senior managers. On the one hand, the project needs to promise enough benefits to engage their backing. On the other hand, it must not over-promise so executive users are easily disappointed. Like most IT projects, not all the benefits will be upfront, so you need to manage their expectations through the project's different stages. If you can deliver some real early benefits, that will give them the confidence to sanction the resources to move on to the next phase.

Choose the appropriate development methods. As we shall see, the traditional method of developing and implementing an IT project does not work very well for executive information systems. In general, a prototype approach works better than conventional system building methodologies. So it is important for the development approach to be decided at the outset as part of the project strategy.

Draw up a realistic budget. Early implementors of executive information systems have not always found it easy to draw up budgets that proved to be accurate. There are horror stories of companies spending more than £1 million on mainframe based systems that ultimately failed to deliver their promised benefits and were abandoned. That is another reason for starting with a more modest project, possibly based on a network of PCs, or mid-range systems.

CHECKLIST 4.3: Costs to be included in the budget

- Third party software
- Communications (i.e. local area networks, modems, etc.)
- Hardware (if new hardware is needed)
- Outside consultancy (if used)
- In-house software tailoring
- Data collection
- Internal project management

- Training
- System support (i.e. hotline etc.)
- Contingency

Finally, it is worth making this point. Selecting and implementing an executive information system is certainly a business issue, but increasingly IT managers are becoming more closely involved at earlier stages in the project. There are two main reasons for this. First, they increasingly recognise the 'political' significance of an executive information system in their companies. They want to be on the inside rather than the outside of such projects. Secondly, they are concerned that the project should dovetail with the company's existing IT strategy, particularly with regard to standards. Again, this is no bad thing, providing the standards are not allowed to stand in the way of a satisfactory business solution.

The Role of Sponsors and Champions

'First catch your hare' – Mrs Beeton's recipe for jugged hare. For someone cooking up an executive information system the advice must be 'first catch your sponsor'. As we have already mentioned the role of sponsors and champions is critical in the success of an executive information system project.

Who should be the sponsor? Ideally, somebody with a vested interest in the success of the system. That probably means somebody who will be using the first application. An executive sponsor is needed for two simple reasons – credibility and clout. First, the project is like no other IT project in your company. As we have seen, it could have a far-reaching impact on the company's management processes. The project could significantly improve the company's competitive edge. It may affect the way different executives relate to one another and the future structure of the company. All this – and the first PCs on the desks of executives who might be far from enthusiastic about the idea. Plainly, then, the executive sponsor needs to be somebody with the credibility to oversee a project at that level and the clout to take the decisions that will be needed.

CHECKLIST 4.4: Sponsors by job title

A study[2] of 36 companies revealed that the sponsors were:

- Chief executive/managing director   10
- Finance directors   14
- Other directors   4
- Other managers   6
- Not known   2

If you are an executive sponsor, what should you do? The first task is to make sure that the proposed executive information system meets real business needs. Much of the success of the project will hinge on other senior executives seeing highly visible benefits from the system at an early stage in the proceedings. As one of those executives, you will have a better idea of the way in which your colleagues think, their preferences and foibles than an equally worthy manager further down the company who rarely treads the thick pile of the executive suite.

Your second task is to take charge of the 'political' elements of the project. It cannot be stated too strongly that an executive information project is not just about sticking PCs on managers' desks. It is about changing the balance of power in the company. Information is about power – someone who has it or can get it more easily has more power; someone who loses control over it has less power. Much of the project is about managing that change in the balance of power. Depending on the complexity of that task and the vested interests in your company that you need to challenge, you could find yourself needing the diplomatic skills of a Henry Kissinger.

Even if there are few 'political' problems in the project, you will still have important tasks to perform. Other senior executives on your level will take the project much more seriously if they can see that 'one of their own' is concerned and committed to it. Introducing an executive information system is not like putting in, say, a stock control system where the clerks in the warehouse don't have much choice over whether they use it or not. On the top floor, senior executives largely determine how they perform their job. So if they decide an executive information system has no part in their working life, they will not use it. Quite simply, they will take more notice of another senior executive than of a systems designer, no matter how brilliant, from the IT department.

Yet even if you perform the role of executive sponsor, providing the much needed credibility and clout to the project, you run a busy working life and cannot be involved with all the details of the day-to-day project management. This is where the project champion comes in. (First, let us just clear away some confusion over terminology. The phrase 'operating sponsor' is sometimes used. Although it is possible to argue that there are some subtle differences between this role and that of project champion, to all intents they are one and the same.)

What kind of person makes the best project champion? Ideally, someone who has many of the qualities of the 'hybrid manager' mentioned in the previous section. He or she will certainly need to be someone who has the complete trust of the project sponsor. (This is a potentially perilous adventure and there can be no doubts between the captain and first mate.) The project champion will need to understand the business implications of the project as well as the technology needed to achieve it.

CHECKLIST 4.5: Champions by job title and department

A study[2] of 36 companies showed that champions were:

- Chief executive/managing director   0
- Directors   7
- Managers   22
- Others   7

The 36 by function were:

- Finance department   12
- IT department   14
- Other departments   10

If you are a project champion, what are your main tasks? Probably the best way to look at your role is as a kind of link between the project sponsor and the project team. You need to manage the project so that it proceeds in a way that ensures the finished executive information system will meet the business needs that were originally identified. In doing this, you will need to understand those needs completely and have a total grasp of the ways in which they are being met within the developing system. You will carry out most of the detailed negotiations with the software suppliers if, as is most likely, you are basing your system on third party software.

If you are using consultants to design part of the system, it will be your task to liaise with them, to explain their tasks and to ensure they are completed to specification and on time. Within your organisation, you will need to liaise with data providers to make sure that the information needed for the executive information system can be made available on time and in the form that is needed. In performing that particular task you will need to take into account the political dimension of obtaining information from other managers as well as the technical difficulties of feeding it into the executive information system. Finally, you need to keep your project sponsor fully aware of the progress of the system and make sure that, among their many other concerns, they do not lose interest or enthusiasm in it.

The project sponsor and the project champion are the two most important people in ensuring the success of an executive information system project. Those managers who have taken on these roles generally say that the tasks are both time-consuming and demanding. Yet champions and sponsors of successful projects say they have derived considerable satisfaction – and in several cases executive kudos – from being involved. Both tasks involve risks, but so does all management, and the prizes, in terms of career advancement, are often greater.

The Different Kinds of Executive Information Systems

There are two ways to get an executive information system. One is to build the system yourself, assembling the different software components from various suppliers. The other is to base your system on third party specialised executive information system software. Despite the perils of doing so, some companies have built their own systems. A notable success story is British Airways, an executive information system pioneer. On the whole, however, that route is fraught with problems. It poses far more technical problems than buying in some third party software would and it leads you to spend much of your time 'reinventing the wheel'. Besides, there is evidence that do-it-yourself systems cost more and stand a greater chance of failure.

If you decide to buy some third party software, you have a choice of different approaches. Moreover, you will probably want to tailor the software you buy to your own special circumstances, and many of the leading packages available on the market are designed with that in mind. There are a number of different ways of looking at executive information systems which can help you to decide which is the best kind of software for your purpose.

The first way is by the different hardware platforms that the software runs on. Broadly speaking, executive information systems can operate on six different kinds of hardware platforms:

Mainframe computers. The executive database is loaded on to the mainframe. It probably has links with database management systems that hold some data. The executive accesses the system through a workstation linked to the mainframe.

Benefits: Access to large amounts of computer power. Close integration with databases holding data.

Drawbacks: the executive information system competes with other mainframe tasks. Potentially expensive development and running costs. Risk of slow response times at executives' terminals when mainframe gets crowded or at busy times.

Mainframe computer and PC. In this case the executive database is loaded onto the mainframe, but executives are provided with PCs on to which they can download part or all of the database they need to work with at any given time. The PC holds the software that enables the executive to work with the downloaded information.

Benefits: Access to large amounts of computer power, coupled with personal and more secure working environment for executive on own PC.

Drawbacks: Expensive approach. Possible slow response in downloading new information sets.

Mid-range system. Such systems now provide as much processing power and data storage capacity as lower-level mainframe computers. They are becoming more popular because they can be used in a decentralised data processing environment and generally impose lower system development and running costs. With the mid-range system, the executive database is held on the mid-range system and information is downloaded to the executives' PCs as and when needed.

Benefits: Plenty of computer power. Lower cost than mainframes.

Drawbacks: Many mid-range systems based on proprietary rather than 'open' operating systems.

Local area network. In this instance the executive database will be held on a 'file server' (generally a powerful PC) in the local area network. Other data may be held on other PCs, or for that matter mainframes or mid-range systems accessible from the network. Executives can access the information they need from their own PC connected to the file server and sometimes from other computers that are accessible.

Benefits: Flexible approach to building a system. Configuration can be changed easily with new users added. Lower cost approach. System can be dedicated to executive information system for security and speed of response.

Drawbacks: Potential delays in accessing really large databases held (possibly for drill-down) on mainframes accessible through file server.

Co-operative processing. In this approach, a collection of PCs are linked together on a network using the 'client-server' technique. The client PCs (in this case, those used by executives) route requests for data to the server PC. This then finds the appropriate slice of data, which could reside on any of the PCs in the network or on an outside computer, such as mid-range system or mainframe (see figure 4.1). The processing of the data that the end-user views is split between the client and the server. Invariably, the client-server approach will use Unix, the open systems operating system that can allow PCs of different makes to be linked together in the same network.

Benefits: Reduced volume of data traffic on the network (only needed data is downloaded to client PCs) which creates faster response times for end-users. Data is processed faster on PCs. Unix can handle much larger files than most other network operating systems, so the executive information systems can grow without technical constraints.

Drawbacks: Very few. But if server goes down, whole network

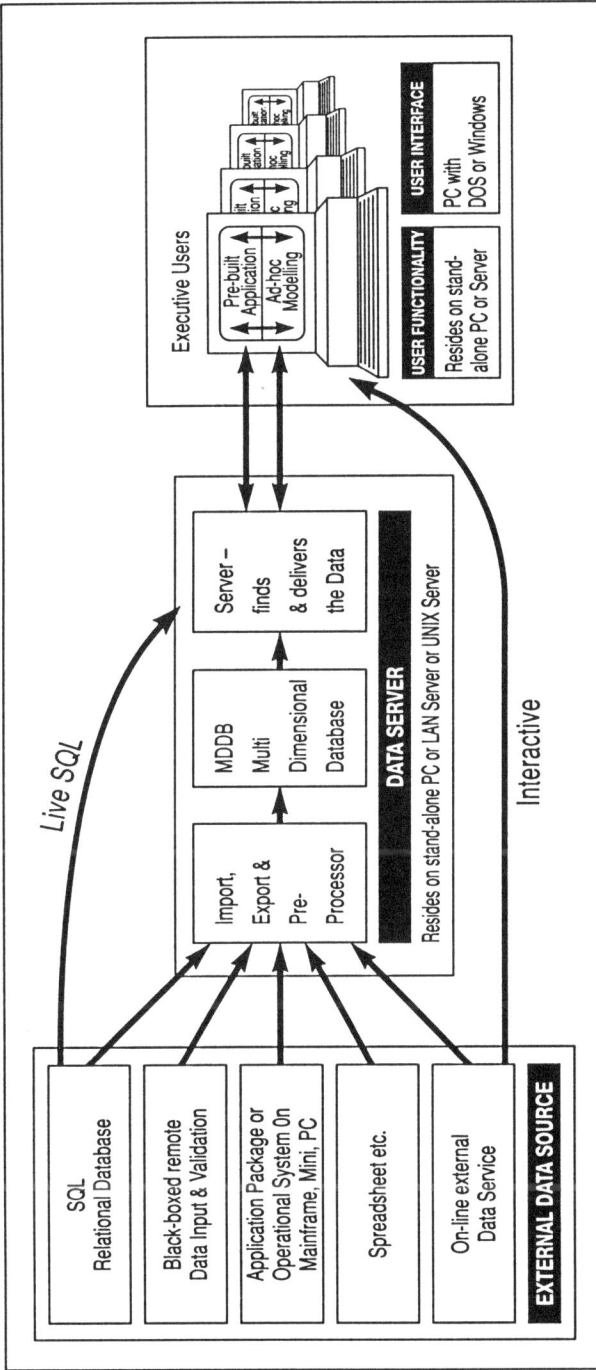

Figure 4.1 Example of a Cooperation Approach

can be incapacitated. (One way to get round this problem is to have a stand-by server.)

Personal computer. In this instance, the executive database is held on a stand-alone computer. Given the nature of the system, it can be used by just one executive at a time.

Benefits: Simple. Low cost. Secure.

Drawbacks: Can only access whatever information is loaded on the PC.

It is dangerous to suggest that one of these approaches is right and the others are wrong. But it is fair to point out that there are some noticeable trends in the market-place. First, given the cost of developing mainframe computer applications, there is a trend away from the mainframe for some applications. More companies are looking at how their computer operations can be 'down-sized' to meet new trading conditions. And down-sizing on to networks using the co-operative processing approach also fits in neatly with the trend towards decentralisation. Increasingly, it seems more sensible for each strategic business unit within a company to have its own discrete information technology facilities – albeit linked over different communication links to other computers in the same company. One reason for this is the increased frequency with which major companies are restructured, with acquisitions, mergers and divestments. In the past, centralised computer facilities, shared by a number of divisions or subsidiaries have often been so difficult to unscramble they have restricted a company's ability to manoeuvre.

The second trend which needs to be mentioned is that towards 'open systems' in which one kind of computer can communicate and exchange information and software freely with another. Although many different hardware manufacturers are moving towards open systems, there is still some considerable distance to go. Even so, the computer makers have achieved enough progress to make open systems an already potent ingredient in decisions about hardware and software choice. Many executive information system software suppliers have recognised the trend towards open systems – and those few that haven't or are too slow to introduce open systems products are likely to find themselves left out in the cold.

The fusion of these two trends is likely to mean that many more companies will be looking at the co-operative processing approach in the future. On the technical side, it combines the two key technical ingredients of information technology for the 1990s

– networks and open systems. On the business side, it provides a means of leveraging existing IT investment, because executive information systems using the technology can be mounted on existing PCs. Finally, from the users' perspective, it provides a simple and straightforward means of accessing an executive information system. Looking to the future, it is an approach that can be developed without any sharp changes of direction.

We have seen, therefore, that looking at the hardware platforms on which executive information systems run is one way of analysing the products in the market-place. Another way you can assess executive information systems is by the way they deliver reports to users. Some systems provide not much more than 'picture shows'. Effectively, pre-formatted screens of data are downloaded into your PC which you can then review in turn. That might be quite useful as far as it goes, but it does not let you investigate the data in depth, because the detail you want to drill-down into may not be held in one of the screens. It also means that the information you are looking at might be out of date unless the data in the screens has been refreshed recently.

The more advanced systems let you perform data-driven reporting. This means that when you want to run a report, the software dives off into the database and extracts the latest information which is fed into the screen of information you want. Generally, it would not matter whether you were viewing the information on screen in numeric or graphical format. Clearly, a data-driven executive information system has considerable advantages over the picture show approach. You view much more up-to-date information and it is also easier to change the format of the reports you want to view. Providing the information is available in the executive database, it will come up on screen.

There is a third reporting approach which is worth noting. That is the ability provided in some executive information system software, to 'browse' in the source databases that supply the executive database. This means that if the information you want is not held in the executive database, you can go off on a data hunt through other corporate databases. That might sound like a wonderful advantage, and it is certainly a useful facility. Nonetheless it is not necessarily as useful as all that. To begin with, most of the information you want to use regularly ought to be in your executive database. Secondly, browsing through databases, such as SQL databases, which you are not familiar with can be a complex process and might be better left to data processing professionals.

In making decisions about the best executive information system software for your company, you need to take decisions about the hardware platform and the way in which the software delivers data to executives. In some cases, decisions about hardware platforms may already be determined by your company's information systems strategy. However, because it is increasingly possible to mount powerful systems on PCs or networks, a growing proportion of users are choosing this route. Links between the PC or network and existing mainframes are built as part of the implementation. As far as the presentation of data is concerned, the 'picture show' executive information system has largely had its day. Most users now want data-driven screens.

In choosing your executive information system, you will need to develop a number of selection criteria. Not all organisations will have the same selection criteria, because they will be governed by factors such as the type of executive information system you plan to select and its objectives. Some of the selection criteria you might want to consider are listed in checklist 4.6.

CHECKLIST 4.6: Executive information system selection criteria

- Users (who are they? where are they? what will they do with the system?)
- Executive database (how big? what kind of information?)
- Executive access (what kind of interfaces? how easy to use?)
- Corporate integration (which existing databases, etc? what links needed to them?)
- Development (how easy to build applications? what tools available?)
- Portability (can applications run on different hardware?)
- Maintenance (how easy to keep system running? what on-going supplier support?)
- Cost (of system? of ownership?)

In a survey[3], 171 companies either using or planning to use an executive information system were asked how important different selection criteria were. Their answers are summarised in checklist 4.7.

CHECKLIST 4.7: Importance of selection criteria

Percentage of companies saying the factor was 'very great' or 'considerable' influence:

• Functionality	93%
• Ease of use	91%
• Ease of development	81%
• Ease of maintenance	75%
• Type of hardware	74%
• Connectivity	69%
• System cost	46%

EXAMPLE: BT

Every organisation should develop selection criteria suited to its own unique circumstances, but BT's approach shows a thorough and structured way of tackling the problem. BT developed a list of 13 selection criteria. Each criterion was weighted. Each product evaluated against the criteria was marked out of ten, then multiplied by the weighting criteria. Finally, totals were added up. The criteria and weightings were:

• Relational database/SQL	10
• Host/PC interface	9
• Multi-dimensional	7
• Drill-down ability	7
• User friendly	10
• Flexibility	10
• Cost	5
• Life cycle stage	5
• Ease of maintenance	7

• BT compatible	3
• Postscript reports	4
• Connectivity	8
• Trend analysis	6

Justifying an Executive Information System

If you were introducing any other kind of computer-based system you would expect to cost-justify it with specific figures. That is a task which is extremely difficult with an executive information system, partly because many of the benefits it delivers are difficult to quantify. That does not mean, however, that you should make no attempt to produce a cost justification for your proposed system at the outset, even though some companies have introduced their systems purely on the basis that it seemed a good idea. Sometimes, those systems have produced good benefits; in other cases, not.

As we have seen from the first section of this chapter, it is possible to produce a fairly accurate estimate of the costs of the first stage of setting up an executive information system. Even so, in order to produce a proper cost-justification, you need to examine not only the set-up costs, but also the costs of ownership. These include continuing support and maintenance from the software supplier, internal staff costs in supporting the system and subscriptions to external data providers if used.

It is important to recognise that the costs of ownership are at least as important, if not more so, than the costs of installing the system. The installation costs are a one-off, the costs of ownership continue month after month, year after year. The biggest single factor in the costs of ownership tends to be the tools used to create the executive information system. If you have installed one of the more complex mainframe-based executive information systems, you could find that the annual costs of ownership will be considerable. Apart from a hefty maintenance charge, you will also need to keep an individual or team of system development professionals in-house to handle new application building. There have been instances where as many as five system staff are supporting a user population of not much more than a dozen–a considerable continuing cost, even if the system is delivering substantial benefits. You will generally find that the PC-based executive information systems will impose lower costs of ownership because they are easier to install and maintain. In addition, new application building is easier.

The cost of an executive information system can vary widely and will be determined by any number of factors. These are:

The kind of system. A large mainframe-based system will cost considerably more than one based on PCs. Costs for mainframe-based systems can run from around £250,000 up to approaching a million.

The number of users. In theory, the more users you have the more the system costs. In practice, comparing expenditure on a cost-per-user basis across sites shows wide variations. There are, for instance, examples of large mainframe-based systems with not more than a couple of handfuls of users where the cost per user runs well into five figures. At the other end of the scale, there are PC-based systems using local area networks with significant user populations rising to 30 or more. In these cases, the cost per user can be in the low four figures. A 1991 study[4] revealed wide disparities. One project with eight users cost £45,000 (£5,625 per user), another with 15 users ran up a bill of £635,000 (£42,333 per user) in 14 months.

The number of applications run. There is a development and on-going support cost for most applications and this will add to basic set-up expenses. Some suppliers provide application templates, but on mainframe systems these can cost as much as £20,000.

The nature of applications run. Some applications cost more to run than others. A major factor is whether the application uses external data. For example, an executive information system in which a range of share prices is updated hourly will clock up a tidy bill to the data user. Other applications will impose a variable system overhead on the computer facilities used depending on the amount of processing power they demand and the traffic of information between databases and the executive information system users.

What kind of benefits can you expect from an executive information system? You need to look at these under two main headings – the benefits which the company as a whole gains and the benefits which executives who use the system gain, although there is a grey area where both overlap.

First, the potential corporate benefits:

Cost savings. Traditionally, this is the first area you might focus on for benefits from IT investment. Nevertheless it is not necessarily the most important area as far as executive information systems are concerned. In many cases it will be quite difficult to point to specific cost displacements, although some users have singled out savings such as redeploying staff employed on compiling and analysing management reports to other tasks.

More effective reporting. This is an area where we start to see some real benefits from executive information systems. If the system cannot present information more effectively than existing paper reports or spreadsheets, then it will be hard to justify at all. In many cases, companies have justified their systems simply on the basis of being able to review existing information more effectively. Yet the benefits ought to extend beyond existing information to providing new information about company performance – information that you could not get from previous reporting systems. In some cases, introducing an executive information system has stimulated a company to redesign its reporting systems to match changing needs. The combination of both areas ought to provide major benefits.

EXAMPLE: Sun Microsystems
Managers at Sun Microsystems, the computer workstation supplier, can now spot trends that previously they might not have noticed for up to three months by using an executive information system. Sales managers used to keep manual reports which were supplemented by monthly information supplied by the finance and marketing departments. Information available through the executive information system is updated nightly. In the morning managers can view the latest data such as sales against targets analysed in different ways, for example by region or customer. Colour graphics add value to the information so that revealing trends can more readily be spotted.

Better understanding of the business. You win this benefit partly through the better reporting processes. You also win by gaining access to more information than you had in the past and the use of tools that enable you to investigate that information when you want to. Executive information system features, such as drill-down and modelling, help you find information you could never get before and analyse it in ways that provide new insights into the way the business is working.

EXAMPLE: London Underground

At London Underground, an executive information system provides senior executives with immediate information about four key areas of the service – trains, station services, finance, safety and security. It is, for example, possible for senior executives to see how many trains ran in the rush hour, a figure which has a big impact on the level of service the Underground will be able to provide during the rest of the day. Executives can obtain information about how long passengers had to wait for trains, failures, delays and incidents.

Introduction of new business processes. As we have seen, managing change is one of the biggest challenges facing business. In this climate, you may need to introduce new business processes more frequently than in the past. Inevitably, this will involve setting up new management structures and designing new information reporting flows to manage the new business processes. In some cases, an executive information system can prove to be an ideal tool for managing such activity.

EXAMPLE: Boots the Chemist

Boots the Chemist, one of the biggest names in British retailing, has switched from its traditional product profitability reporting system to a new 'direct product profitability' strategy. Under the old system, the profit made on each product was calculated by subtracting the cost price from the sale price. Under the new system, the true profit made on each product is calculated after taking account of costs such as warehousing, transport, sales space and other factors. The new strategy gives Boots' executives a much clearer picture of where it earns its profits, but the system generates huge amounts of information. Senior managers use an executive information system to access and analyse the information.

Improved ability to solve problems. The problem with problems is that you never have enough information or enough time to solve them. That makes finding a solution doubly difficult. An executive information system cannot solve problems by itself, but it gives you a better chance of solving them in two ways. First, it gives you access to more relevant information more quickly. Secondly, it lets you test different possible solutions before selecting the best one. That means you don't have to adopt the first possibility that seems half sensible but can explore more and imaginative answers. Sometimes, the best answer is one you did not expect. The executive information system helps you find it.

EXAMPLE: British Airways

British Airways found its pioneering executive information system of special value after slumps in trans-Atlantic bookings following the Libyan bombing in 1986 and the Gulf war in 1991. In both cases, executives used the system to model business patterns and the likely timetable of bookings revival. This gave executives the confidence to launch aggressive marketing strategies aimed at winning a larger market share during the slump, rather than cutting back on capacity like competitors.

Next, what benefits can executives expect? Here the problem of quantifying benefits becomes, if anything, even tougher. But there are a number of areas worth looking at when justifying an executive information system.

Time saving. You will probably not find you have more spare time if you install an executive information system. However, you will be able to perform some routine tasks, such as reviewing periodic reports, more quickly. Alternatively, you can spend the same time as before, but gain greater insights into the information through spending your time analysing the information rather than looking for it.

EXAMPLE: British Rail Network SouthEast

Engineers in the Infrastructure division of Network SouthEast plan and allocate resources to each of the maintenance projects in each of Network SouthEast's seven divisions. Yet frequently they had inadequate information to make decisions, and trying to find the information wasted hours with phone calls. Now an executive information system provides data by resource, time and location to help managers plan. In addition, head office can gain an overview of the planning process to ensure resources are being allocated most effectively.

Less paper. Again, you will not notice an appreciable reduction in the amount of paper hitting your desk; but some reports that used to arrive on paper will now be accessible through the screen. When you get used to the system, you will find it easier to get information from your screen than from a paper report.

EXAMPLE: Babcock Energy

Managers found it difficult to find and interpret production information from a mass of paper reports and other sources. The solution was to install an executive information system which presents much of the information on-screen in graphics charts which help to highlight the key issues which managers need to address. The result is that the flow of information has been speeded up. In addition, introduction of the executive information system highlighted a number of shortcomings in Babcock's existing information which managers were able to rectify.

Improved communications. You gain improved communications in two ways: information reaches you more promptly; and you can communicate with colleagues more easily if you have access to their workstations across a network. The fact that managers know they are due to report information through the system tends to provide more discipline, so fewer reports arrive late. As the managers know their report will have a higher visibility through your workstation than it would on paper, they tend to take more care over its accuracy and presentation. You can have your executive information system provided with a number of semi-standard memos to send to colleagues. Combined with an ability to extract information from screens easily, this provides a quicker and easier method of inter-office communication than dictating memos to a secretary.

EXAMPLE: Oki Europe

Oki Europe is a Japanese-owned computer product manufacturer, best known for its printers. It operates in ten European countries and managers were finding it difficult to collect information about products and financial results from each country. The answer was an executive information system installed in Oki's London head office and the ten country offices. In each of the country offices, information about

---

products and financial results is input to the system. That data is used to provide local managers with monthly information. It is also passed to London for consolidation and review. Now, managers all over Europe can interrogate information that promotes a common view of the data. When a senior manager from head office visits a country, he can access information in the same format as everywhere else, which makes it easier to understand and review.

More effective meetings. Increasingly, executive information systems are being used in groups so that managers can review facts together and develop a shared perception of a situation. In those circumstances, you will probably discover you spend less time arguing about the facts of the situation – you all share the same information – and more time discussing the significance of the information and the action you need to take.

5

HOW TO IMPLEMENT AN
EXECUTIVE INFORMATION SYSTEM

'If you don't know where you are going, you will probably
end up somewhere else.'
>   – Laurence J. Peter, *The Peter Principle*

Choosing the First Application

We have looked at the business forces at work that generate the
need for executive information systems. We have examined the
ways in which you should set about choosing executive information system software. Now how do you choose your first application? You need to bear in mind the points made in earlier
chapters: executive information systems are different in many
respects from other IT applications your company may have
implemented.

The core point to consider right at the outset is that while the
application is going to deliver benefit to the business as a whole, it
is going to be used (initially) by an individual or small group of
individuals. This means that the chosen application must address
what those individuals see as a key business issue for the
company. This changes the perspective for most people used to
delivering IT applications.

You normally start from the business problem and produce a
system that will be used by people to help solve that problem.
Often, with lower level IT applications, staff don't have much say
in whether they are going to use the application or not. That is not
the case with an executive information system. If the executive
information system starts off at the highest levels of the company,

the users will have plenty of say over whether or not they want to use it. So in developing the system, you need to start by looking through the other end of the telescope and asking: 'What does the individual want?'.

That individual wants to solve a specific business problem, probably made worse by information overload. Yet unless the solution you provide tackles the problem from his or her specific perspective, it will very likely not succeed. In a way, the difference between conventional IT system development and creating an executive information system is rather like the difference between a speculative housing estate and an architect designed house. When you buy an already built house, you find one that matches your needs as nearly as possible, move in, carry out some alterations and make the most of it. With an architect designed house, you not only specify the features you want from the outset, you say where you want it built and how those features are to be arranged. In this respect, the future user of an executive information system is rather like the person commissioning an architect designed house.

There are a number of important considerations to bear in mind when choosing the first executive information system application.

Targeted. The executive information system is more likely to succeed if it is targeted at solving a specific and identified business problem. It is tempting to imagine that a system will earn its keep simply by presenting information to the user in a more effective and digestible way. While that may be true, an executive information system introduced only to improve the presentation of existing management information will not win the biggest benefits and may not sustain the commitment of the end-user. You will convince senior executive users of the benefit payoff of the system if you can show that it will provide real answers to very specific problems.

Clear objectives. It follows that if you have targeted a specific application, you need to develop clear objectives for what you want it to achieve. In other words, you need to identify the benefits you expect the system to deliver. As we have seen, the benefits in an executive information system are as likely to be 'soft' as 'hard' and it may, therefore, be more difficult to express them. However that does not mean you should not make every effort to do so with the assistance of the future user of the system. In working with the user to identify the benefits he or she wants, you will gain a clearer idea of the scope of the application, the kind of information it will need to deliver and the range of features it will have to offer. You will also gain a valuable insight into the character and working practices of the potential user. This will help you to style the application to the user. You need to go through this exercise with each of the executive users because each user will want the application specifically styled for their own needs.

Early results. As we have seen, top executives are impatient people who like to get results quickly. It makes sense, therefore, to choose a first application where you can show some quick benefits. If you have targeted an application tightly enough and developed clear objectives with the prospective users, you should be able to see ways of structuring the development process so that you deliver some high profile benefits early on in the development. An extra benefit of delivering early results is that it helps to win executive commitment for the next stages of the project.

Prototype development. Even if you have targeted an application and identified benefits, you will still find that, in the nature of executive information systems, there are some grey areas. This makes the prototyping approach to application development particularly attractive in this area. With a prototype, you can develop an outline system to enable the executive user to get an idea of its 'look and feel'. In this way, the application building proceeds step by careful step with plenty of user feedback at every stage.

EXAMPLE: BP Chemicals
Ken Greenslade, executive information systems project manager at BP Chemicals, adopted these rules for prototyping:
- Use live data
- Present data that is available through other routes
- Run as an operational system
- Encourage feedback
- Monitor use of the system

Capable of growth. You wouldn't be involved with executive information systems unless you felt they had a long term future with your company. This means you want to choose a first application where there is plenty of potential for further growth. When top executives see success, they want to build on it. Fast. It is in their nature to want to be constantly moving forward. You want to avoid the 'Is that it?' syndrome. After a few months, you don't want your executive information system to seem as dull as last year's Christmas present. That means you need to have an eye to growth potential even when you choose your first application area.

Low risk. As we have seen, implementing an executive information system can be a high risk business. So don't add to that risk by choosing a high risk application for your first. There is no reason why you have to climb Everest the hard way in your first ascent. In seeking a low risk application, look for one where the boundaries of the application are clear, where the benefits are as hard as possible, and where you are sure the underlying data needed to support the application is (mostly) available. It is also important to understand that you reduce the risk by having an executive user who has firm enthusiasm for the project, a sense of realism about the difficulties of implementing it and a commitment to spend the time needed to make it succeed.

We have seen above some of the *characteristics* of a successful first executive information system application. But what about the *subject* of it? That needs to be related both to the needs of the business and to those of the user executive. It will also deliver benefit if the application deals with a topic that is essential to the success of the business.

One way to do this is to identify the critical success factors of the business and the key performance indicators that help you to judge whether you are meeting your critical success factors. The idea of the critical success factor goes back to the mid-1960s; but the concept first started receiving serious attention from executives in the early 1980s, following John Rockart's 1979 *Harvard Business Review* article 'Chief executives define their own data needs.'[1] In that article, Rockart suggested a company's critical success factors were the 'limited number of areas in which results, if they are satisfactory, will ensure successful competitive performance for the organisation'.

In practical terms, the critical success factors are, themselves, driven by the company's goals. In a large organisation, each division or subsidiary may well have its own set of critical success factors which contribute to its success and feed into the overall performance of the whole organisation (see figure 5.1). The importance of critical success factors is that they can help to guide you to areas for the first application. Of course, the critical success

Figure 5.1

Critical Success Factors

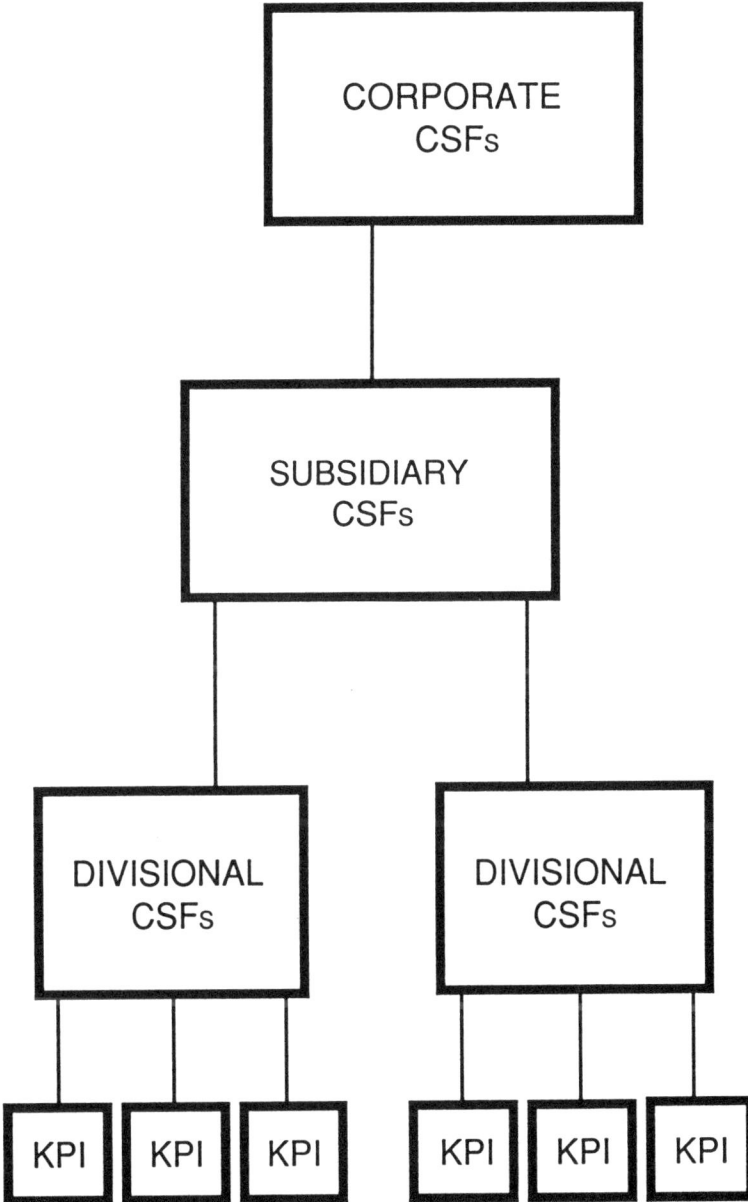

CSF Critical Success Factor KPI Key Performance Indicator

factors must be developed before you can do that, a task which involves substantial involvement from senior management.

CHECKLIST 5.1: Five important features of a critical success factor

- Measureable
So you can tell, by measuring with key performance indicators, whether you achieve it

- Regularly updated
So it remains relevant

- Relevant
So that it actually drives the success of the organisation

- Comparable
So that it can be related to desired standards of achievement

- Actionable
So that managers can take action to make sure it is achieved

EXAMPLE: British Steel Distribution.
BSD undertook a structured exercise to identify critical success factors before it introduced an executive information system. The CSFs it identified included:
- Management of working capital
- Product differentiation, measured by indicators such as gross margin and market share
- Cost monitoring
- Acceptable return, measured by indicators such as return on capital employed and ratios such as the profit before tax related to sales

You should review your company's existing CSFs or give serious consideration to developing new CSFs in conjunction with senior executives before embarking on any executive information system application. However, while CSFs are extremely valuable as a guide to targeting an application area, and the key performance indicators lead you towards the kind of information the executive information system needs to capture and present, the two between them provide just a framework for the application (see figure 5.1). Before you can build the application with confidence, you will need to find out more about precisely what each individual user wants from the application and how each proposes to use it. In doing this, you can adopt a number of different approaches:

Structured interviewing of users.

Method: Develop an interview framework in conjunction with others involved in the project and the proposed interviewee. Then take each proposed user through the interview, recording information in detail.

Advantages: Focuses on the perceived issues in a logical way. Ensures all information is systematically recorded.

Drawbacks: The framework may be incomplete through missing out more personal issues.

Interviewing around users.

Method: Interview business analysts, assistants and colleagues who work with the prospective user to get their perspective on what he or she does and the information he or she uses.

Advantages: Obtains a rounded picture from different perspectives.

Drawbacks: Misses the user's personal perspective on key application issues.

Fly on the wall.

Method: Shadow the executive over a period of time, to obtain a view of his or her work flows, information needs and decision-making processes as well as working style.

Advantages: Provides picture of the executive's current working style.

Drawbacks: May miss important clues about what he or she would like in the future.

It is, of course, possible to use a combination of the above methods. That could considerably add to the work involved in identifying needs, but would provide a more rounded picture. Given the vital importance of identifying executive needs correctly, you should not skimp on the amount of time you put into this part of the project.

EXAMPLE: Yorkshire Building Society

Yorkshire Building Society wisely decided to develop its executive information system in phases. Equally wisely, the development team set out some ground rules with the

---

executives before the development started. Maureen Worsman, who was closely involved with the systems development, explains:

'First, we decided not to use current information as a basis for making decisions on what our system would consist of. Secondly, we agreed what the executives expected of me and what I expected of them; the responsibilities were, therefore, identified and accepted. Thirdly, we all agreed to walk before we could run and not expect too much too soon. Fourthly, we agreed initial deadlines that we felt were achievable and also planned how progress would be reported.'

Worsman adds: 'Without these ground rules the system could not have developed in the most effective way.' Worsman identified the information needs for phase one of the project by designing a series of questions that were aimed at allowing executives to talk about their role within the Society and identify their perceived critical success factors. From that, it was possible to identify what information was needed to meet those success factors. Although some executives had some difficulty in identifying their information requirements, they were clear about the major areas of information they needed. Worsman explains:

'For this reason, we decided to develop the information models containing the main items of information they would wish to analyse. We would then leave the defining of the precise viewing format until later. This has enabled the executives to use the information models to form clearer opinions on the format – including charts. Our executives found this a refreshing change to the traditional way of developing systems.'

Worsman's team had to find out how easy it would be to develop the information before making final decisions with the executives. They also had to agree on how frequently the information would be updated. This process created much lively discussion about the purpose of the information. All decisions were recorded, but Worsman says: 'We did not use the usual chunky documentation style for traditional projects as this would have taken too much time and was not necessary.' She adds: 'An executive information systems project not only identifies the information requirements, but also develops the executives' views of information. It can, therefore, be challenging for them.'

CHECKLIST 5.2: Some typical first executive information system applications

Motor car manufacturer:	Operational statistics for quality monitoring
Clearing bank:	Monthly management accounts with exception reporting by business unit
Food manufacturer:	Presentation of financial data to non-accounting senior management
Energy utility:	Board-level performance monitoring
Furniture retail chain:	Monitoring performance against competitors
Brewer:	Tracking performance of brand sales
Consumer goods manufacturer:	On-line monitoring of production machinery performance

The Political Dimension

All change creates winners and losers. Executive information systems are all about managing change. Therefore when an executive information system is introduced in an organisation there will be winners and losers. QED. Because the 'political' issues involved in introducing an executive information system are so important, there is no point in not facing up to this important truth. Indeed, by facing up to it, you can identify the issues that are likely to cause shifts in the management power structure, so that you can effectively manage them. You should be in no doubt about the risks of sidelining the political is-sues – you will create a situation in which some people have a vested interest in keeping things as they are and not helping the success of your executive information project. Keynes[2] said: 'In the long run it is ideas, not vested interests, that are dangerous for good or for evil.' Your problem is that you are introducing an executive information system in the short run so it is the vested interests that start with the upper hand.

The critical political issue to manage is the change in information flows generated by your executive information system. Those flows could create a significant shift in the existing management power structure. In most cases, the impact of an executive information system is to give people at the top much more direct access to information further down the management hierarchy. This has two important spin-off effects.

First, business analysts and paper shufflers feel threatened. In most organisations, there will be around each executive a cadre of management NCOs whose task is to seek out, analyse and present regular data to their chief. When an executive information system appears, this group, like the ruling classes in Marxist theory, start to wither away. At best, their role – and, therefore, their influence over their chief – becomes less important. At worst, they are out of a job. The problem for you as an executive information system implementor is that these people have a vast residue of wisdom about the flow of information that reaches their chief and the way in which he or she takes decisions. If they choose, they can join the awkward squad and make life difficult for you.

The only way to deal with this problem is to be open and honest with them at the outset. You need to explain what you are doing, why it is important and what the new system's role will be. In some cases, the analysts may actually have an enhanced role after the introduction of the executive information system. (They may spend more time analysing information rather than just collecting it.) In other cases, their role will diminish or even disappear. Whichever is the case, they need to be treated properly. Often analysts can be found another role in the organisation and paper shufflers can find there are more interesting functions in a working life than shuffling paper. This may all sound rather like buying off people who will no longer be needed in their current role. Put bluntly, it is. However if the executive information system delivers the overall benefits you expect, it will be a price well worth paying.

Second, line managers at lower levels in the organisation. Here you could encounter a range of potential political problems. Line managers, like business analysts, may have played an information massaging role for senior executives. Again, this role may no longer be needed. Even more fundamentally, it will not take long for it to dawn on line managers that the old practice of handing up information summaries to senior executives effectively rationed the information the top people received. There is little or no rationing with an executive information system. This may make line managers feel as exposed as the song-writer's girl with the 'itsy-bitsy teeny-weeny yellow polka-dot bikini'.

In some cases, a greater openness and exposure will be no bad thing. Experience shows that the introduction of an executive information system will reveal some departments that are, frankly, not conducting a satisfactory information gathering and record keeping regime. The exposure provided by an executive information system will encourage them to clean up their act. In other cases, information systems will be in apple pie order. In that instance, it is important for the system developer and executive users to make clear to the line managers at the outset that the access to information will be used responsibly. As the management guru David De Long[3] put it in a conference speech: 'You shouldn't use information to beat people up'. Indeed, by using information responsibly, it is actually possible to make line managers feel closer to the decision-making heart ('Those sales figures were interesting, Joe, what do you feel we should do about them?') than they did before. Some of the time saved by both parties should be used to discuss together the implications of the information provided and accessed.

Over all these issues hangs the question of 'data ownership'. Managers at whatever level who have responsibility for collecting information about their activities do not like to feel that their responsibility is being taken over. So you need to make it clear from the start that an executive information system is not about usurping 'their' information. Indeed, because the information becomes more regularly used and more vital in the decision-making process, their custodianship of it becomes even more important.

What you must do if you are to manage the political aspects of an executive information system is to create a co-operative development culture right through the organisation. Even if the first application is only to be used directly by a small number of senior users, everybody who contributes to it must be told how their role plays a part in the success of the project. You will find that a co-operative development culture will emerge if everybody involved feels there are advantages all around. Benefits, like manure, are most effective when they are spread about. Even though some of the most significant benefits, from the corporate point of view, will be gained at the top, there could be benefits right down the management chain (a reduction in the number of monthly reports to be prepared, for instance).

In short, let everybody involved have a slice of the benefits and you will find they will all be working for the system's success.

Developing the First Application

Building an executive information system in an evolutionary way, step by careful step, is not only desirable but essential. You should also build each of the applications within the executive information system in an evolutionary way. Just what are the main features of an evolutionary application? You need to take on board two important points. First, even if you can see at the outset the whole picture of the finished application, you need to make a conscious decision not to leap to that point in one step. For executive information systems developers, fired with enthusiasm, that may involve some restraint. Alternatively, the picture of the finished application may not be clear to you. Even so, the first steps towards it are. In this case, building the first step of the application will help to clarify what you need for subsequent steps.

It is not the technology, as such, but the nature of the executive users which makes the evolutionary approach so desirable. Few executives will admit to not knowing what information they want. Nevertheless when it comes down to defining their needs in detail, many find it hard to specify precisely what they are. One reason for this is that executives often use information in random and unstructured ways. It is also frequently not clear what information they actually need in order to take a specific decision. As executive information system pioneer David De Long points out, executives 'don't think about their business through an information lense'. They also don't know what the computer's capabilities are or have any clear objectives for an executive information system.

Because executives want quick results, the initial scope of the first application needs to be limited. What do we mean by quick

90

results? In some companies, delivering the first application a year after deciding to go ahead has been reckoned pretty nifty, but the real Speedy Gonzales have presented first (very basic) applications in as little as four weeks. The central truth is that an executive is more likely to support a slim application that looks as though it might be going places rather than a promised all-singing all-dancing application that is forever stuck in development.

In an evolutionary implementation there are six main steps; but whereas in a conventional computer system these will be more or less discrete, in an executive information system they overlap (see figure 5.2). The six steps are:

Step 1: Define user needs. Plainly the first step, but as the success of the application will depend on it, it is wise to spend as much time as possible on this phase.

Step 2: Specify functions. This flows logically from defining user needs. You will find that as you specify the specific functions in the system, the user will think of new needs. This means you need to be prepared for a certain blurring of the edges between these first two steps.

Step 3: Decide on architecture. This involves deciding on which of the architectural approaches described in chapter 4 is the right one for your executive information system. You also need to look at the question of data delivery – discovering where the data you need to drive the application resides and deciding how it will be delivered into the executive database.

Step 4: Design components. At this stage you design the screens and supporting software needed to deliver the application to the end user.

Step 5: Presentation and review. At this point, you present the first prototype of the application to the end-user. It should run using live data, but it need not offer all the functionality you plan to include. The aim is to see whether you are thinking along the same lines as the end-user. It also gives you the chance to get feedback from the user which can then be incorporated into the system.

Step 6: Roll-out and training. Now the first version of the application is rolled out to executives for live use. The application should be designed so the user can understand how to operate it with no more than about half an hour's training, and preferably less. Within days, you should be seeking feedback from the user on the application so that you can incorporate user-driven improvements

Figure 5.2

Prototyping an Executive Information System

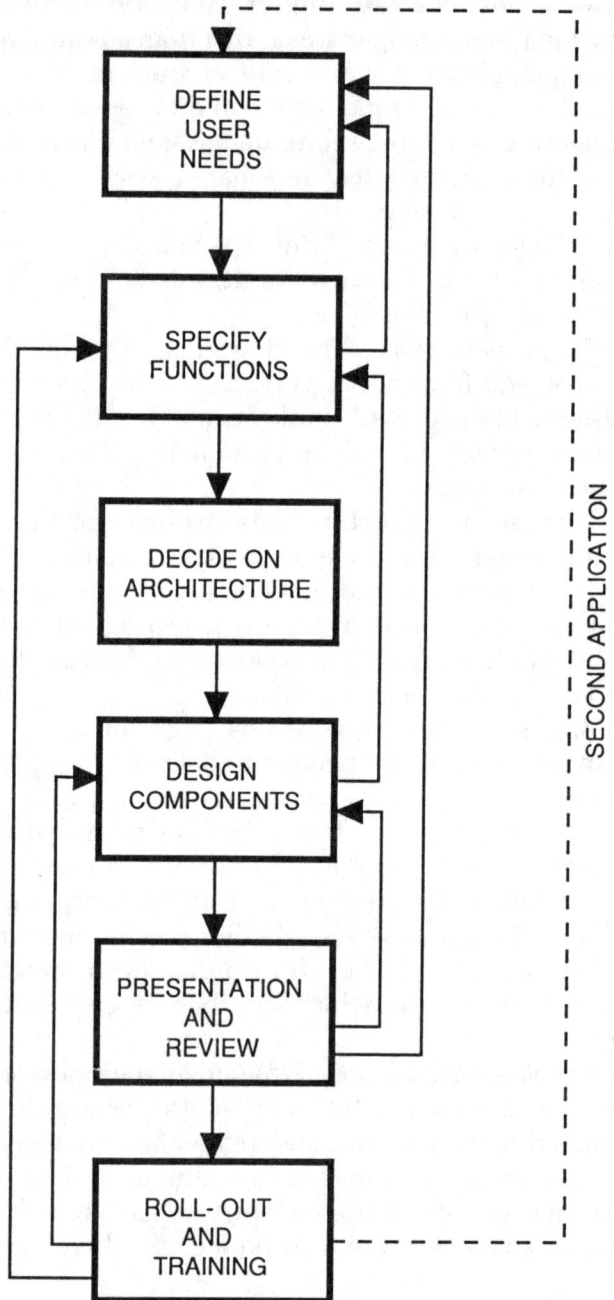

and suggestions into it. As you can see, this evolutionary approach uses what is, broadly, a prototyping approach to the application's development.

CHECKLIST 5.3: Seven rules for prototyping an executive information system

David De Long[3] recommends these rules for an effective 'adaptive prototyping' approach to system building:

* Set realistic deadlines
* Anticipate data problems
* Take time and commitment to get value
* Prioritise applications
* Expect varying responses
* Customise, customise
* Create and adapt – seek honest feedback

One of the main problem areas in building an application is defining and collecting the data that you want to incorporate in it. Indeed, in not a few cases, it is the problems with data that have stopped companies building an executive information system. If yours is a company which has built decision support models based on 'clean' and consistent data, you will have a head start when you begin building your executive information system. Although even if you are beset by problems of non-existent, inconsistent and 'dirty' data, you can still build an executive information system. The data problems will exist whether you build the system or not, and the fact of building the system can draw top management's attention to them. Often, this produces the commitment to devote resources to sorting them out.

CHECKLIST 5.4: Achieving consistent data presentation

Peter King[4], managing director of Campion Associates, a consultancy specialising in executive information system assignments, provides these tips for cleaning up dirty data:

* Check accuracy

- Clarify definitions
- Detail responsibility centres
- Check accounting treatment
- Describe assumptions
- Establish change mechanisms
- Obtain data owner, data user and data supplier views
- Assign responsibility for consistency

It might be nice to think that new users of executive information systems set out to find an application they have always wanted but have never been able to perform. In the real world, many first executive information system applications are based on existing paper reports. There are both opportunities and dangers in this situation. The opportunity is that because executives are already familiar with the paper reports they can see the relevance of the application. Also, if the data is in paper reports it must exist. The danger is that if the application does no more than replicate columns of figures – similar to those in the reports – on the executives' screens, they will soon wonder why they bothered to agree to the application and lose interest in it.

The key to all successful executive information system applications is in adding value to the data. Ways in which you can add value to data are listed in the checklist below.

CHECKLIST 5.5: Ways of adding value to data

Quicker delivery:	Time between close of reporting period and delivery of data is reduced
More regular update:	Information is updated more often than in paper-based reports
Colour:	Colour is used to make information more presentable and easier to follow (note: this can be done with figures as well as charts and graphs)

Exception reports:	System is programmed to highlight figures that do not conform to the expected
Variance reports:	System is programmed to highlight figures that are above or below given variances. More than one variance can be shown simultaneously on the same screen
Charts and graphs:	Figures can be automatically charted or graphed in a variety of ways
Maps:	Figures can be presented on maps (for example, sales from different sales territories)
Drill-down:	Users can investigate the make up of any aggregated figure on the screen
Ratios:	Users can measure the ratios between different sets of figures or chart the ratios
Trends and projections:	Users can see past patterns and project past performance into the future
Hot spots:	Quick ways for the manager to access regularly much-used figures or ratios

You will find that the techniques described in checklist 5.5 are not the only ways you can add value to the executive information system and thus increase executive commitment to using it. For example, although most first applications usually concentrate on using internal data, the executive information system can soon be made to deliver some form of external data – perhaps key share prices or relevant news headlines. Indeed, introducing some regularly updated information into the system is important, especially for a system whose first application is standard financials. Most corporate financials are updated only once a month, but if the executive information system is to have a growing future, you want managers to use it more regularly. They should not get into a habit of looking on the system as something that comes into its own on the first Tuesday of the month or whenever.

Other ways of adding value to an executive information system are listed in checklist 5.6.

CHECKLIST 5.6: How to add value to an application

Authorship:	Put the name of the manager providing the information in the corner of each screen
Variety:	Don't let screens get stale. Have information changing all the time – such as the date the information was last updated
Easy access:	Provide short-cuts for each manager to the screens he or she uses most
Bulletin board:	Provide a company bulletin board screen in the application
Alert:	Provide an automatic on-screen alert when important information arrives in the system
Intelligent newspaper:	Provide a service of news items filtered from a news provider (i.e. *Financial Times*) by key word searches
Quick memos:	Provide semi-standard memos for quick inter-company messages

---

Whichever application is chosen, you need to bear in mind a final important lesson if it is to be successful. The application needs to be personalised for each individual user. For example, one user might want to access a particular screen more often than another user. Therefore he or she needs a quick route (see checklist) to help get to that screen. One manager might want to look at a screen of information in figures, another in graphs and another in both. The screens need to be tailored to individual uses. The more you make the system seem like a personal work and productivity tool for individual executives, the more they are likely to use it; and that increases its chances of growing and delivering real business benefits.

CHECKLIST 5.7: How to build a successful executive information system

David Thomas[5], an executive information system specialist at Andersen Consulting, gives these nine critical success factors for a project:

- Obtain and nurture executive commitment
- Manage executive expectations
- Understand and address management and political issues
- Be sure the system adds value
- Use appropriate products
- Employ a skilled project team
- Do not compromise on quality
- Focus on data sourcing and integrity
- Manage change

The Fall-out on the Organisation

Introducing the first executive information system is like throwing a stone into a perfectly still mill pond. There is a splash and then the ripples start to reach out right to the edge of the pond. The system will have an impact on the organisation as a whole as well as the top executives using it.

One of the biggest impacts, you will find, is on corporate reporting practices. Quite simply, for the executive information system to work, executives must share the same data. We have already mentioned the problem of 'dirty data'. A common effect of this is that different executives end up looking at different figures. The result is that before any meaningful discussion can take place, you need to argue about who has the 'right' figures. With an executive information system, you all have the same figures, so that problem is removed.

That, by itself, is a substantial benefit, but you may find that as the executive information system seeps into your corporate culture, it confers other more subtle and unexpected changes. For example, your executives have always used 'information' in their working lives, probably without thinking too much about it. The fact that they didn't think about it much means they probably didn't attach much value to the information. Often, introducing an executive information system throws a spotlight on the fact that information is a valuable corporate resource, which ought to be cherished and carefully managed.

Now, as the executive information system makes the same data available to everyone, you may find that a new information culture emerges in your company. You want to encourage a culture that emphasises sharing rather than witholding. As the new culture emerges, executives should increasingly see information as a resource to be used creatively in order to achieve future business success. Developing such a co-operative information culture can be worth the price of an executive information system itself.

You could also find that an executive information system imposes more rigorous information collection and reporting practices on your company. Like regular exercise and early nights, the system is good for you. For example, you may find that you need to adopt company-wide procedures and standards for databases. You may need to adopt standards for the way in which data is recorded – for example, for time series or currency conversion – so that the same data means the same thing whichever part of the company it comes from.

On top of all that, you may find that the executive information system will open the eyes of managers to the amount of understanding that can simply be released from the information. One quite common feature of this is the way in which managers suddenly realise that figures which had been presented for years in columns on paper reports without any explanation, need some kind of written explanation if they are to be fully understood and interpreted. When an executive information system takes off, you will find managers at all levels spurred to find ways to present information in more meaningful ways.

An executive information system is unusual among computer systems in that it is never finished. It is true that most business systems are updated on a regular timescale. The point about an executive information system is that it is updated more or less continuously. Indeed, the system that is not being constantly updated and expanded is probably dead in the water, for senior executive users will soon become bored with it.

One of the spin-off effects of constantly updating executive information systems is that they are extremely difficult to document. The documentation can be out of date as soon as you have created it. Some users have found that a more viable strategy is to document how you do things – for example, how you describe different classifications of data, or conventions used in graphs and charts – rather than to try to keep a detailed documentation of the whole system. Even so, you would be well advised to keep at least a list of screens available to each user as a kind of outline map of the system.

EXAMPLE: How ICI's executive information system continues to grow
1986 (April) Prototype
1986 (September) 5 users; 4 modules
1987 (September) Chairman becomes 10th user
1988 (April) 18 users including 4 directors
1989 (March) 60 users including 7 directors
1991 (October) 140 users including 7/9 directors; 80 modules

Before you set out on a determined policy to grow your executive information system, you need to develop a framework to assess the value the first application is delivering to the executives who use it. You will probably find you can assess this benefit in two main areas; the personal advantage the system delivers to the executives and the measurable, bottom-line benefits the system delivers to the company as a whole. In some cases, the former is easier to quantify than the latter, although there are one or two startling anecdotes about how executives claim to have made millions for their companies using an executive information system.

In some cases, you may find that executives develop unbounded enthusiasm about their system. In other cases, the response is more muted. In both, the executives may be gaining benefit. Whichever is the case, it is worth making a structured effort to tease out from executives the kind of benefits they feel they gain from the system. (As a side effect of this exercise, you will gain information about areas where the information flow or system features could be improved.) Probably the best way to gain this information is through a formal structured interview rather than informal chats, if only because it emphasises the importance of the exercise and forces both parties – the user and the system developer – to focus their minds on the issue. When you conduct the interview depends partly on how quickly your executive users adopt the system. Nevertheless there is considerable value in having the first interview quite early, perhaps as soon as a month after the executive has started to use the system. An early interview will let you gain first impressions and pick up any problems before they have time to get out of hand.

If your executive information system is to grow, it ought to do so in a planned rather than an unplanned way. You need to give thought to: how the system for existing users will be expanded; and who will be allowed on to the system as new users.

Answers to the first question will partly come from your continuing contact with the first users. They will soon tell you what new information and features they want built into their application. They may also have their own ideas about what the next applications ought to be. Even so, you have limited resources and cannot do everything at once. You need to develop priorities for who is getting what and when. In fact, you need an agreed approach to prioritising requests for new work. There is a strong case for involving the executive users in developing this policy, perhaps through setting up a steering group. Some users may have conflicting priorities and it is important that they should agree them among themselves. As a system sponsor or developer, you should strongly resist being dragged into backstairs politicking.

The second question – which new users should have access to the system – certainly needs a clear policy. Moreover, it needs to be a policy which is driven by business needs. If the first application is successful, there could well be a strong demand from other executives who feel shut off from important flows of information. You need to decide whether you want to restrict the use of the executive information system to senior users or whether, in the long run, you want it spread down to middle manager levels. Some companies have taken the view that the system should be kept exclusive. Yet they are probably swimming against an increasingly strong tide. If an executive information system delivers benefits, it makes sense to bring those benefits to as many managers as can sensibly gain them. However if you take a decision in principle you still need to decide who will obtain access to the system first. Plainly, that decision must be driven by where the greatest business benefit can be gained most quickly.

6

HOW TO USE AN EXECUTIVE
INFORMATION SYSTEM

'Get your facts first, and then you can distort them as much
as you please.'

– Mark Twain

Start with the Basics

If a manager needs an extensive training course before being able
to use his or her executive information system, the system is
doomed from the start. In an ideal world, the system would be so
intuitive and easy to use that no training at all would be needed.
In the real world, the executive information system developer has
to face the harsh fact that there are people who have reached the
top seat in major public companies without knowing how to turn
on a PC. In many cases, there are two main purposes to the
training: to remove the 'technofear' from a manager who has
never encountered a PC before; and to get the user started by
talking him or her through the means of accessing the system and
the ways of navigating around the screens.

Overall, the training should have the same tone as a motor car
salesman showing a customer the features of a new car he or she
has never driven before. Indeed, there is an element of salesman-
ship in the training in that you want to enthuse the manager to
use the features of the new executive information system.

One big obstacle stands in the way of training top executives.
Their egos. If you are the system implementor you are in a
delicate position, rather like a lowly lieutenant telling General
Montgomery how to win the war in the western desert. Therefore

two of the most important qualities you need are diplomacy and tact. First, it is a good idea to get rid of the word 'training' which carries connotations of master and pupil. Better phrases to use are 'introductory session', 'commissioning session', or 'familiarisation'.

Secondly, you want to conduct the training in such a way that the executive will not look a fool if he or she gets something wrong. A problem with many top executives is that they have a very low embarrassment threshold. They don't like to be seen making mistakes in front of subordinates – after all, those lesser mortals might think they are only human. It follows that you need to conduct all training on a one-to-one basis. In any event, if you have customised the system to the needs of each executive, you will have to show each one separately how to use it. So group sessions for all new system users are most definitely out.

Thirdly, the really top executives of the largest companies rely on a small praetorian guard of secretaries and personal assistants to perform their common daily tasks for them. It could make sense to ensure the key members of their personal staff know how to operate the system, too. Who do executives turn to when they want to know something? Their secretaries. So train the secretaries. However make sure you do this in separate sessions after you have trained the executives. (They will not take kindly to their secretaries knowing more about the system than they do.)

Finally, set up some form of 'hotline' support service that executives and their secretaries can turn to. Make the hotline proactive. This is one case where no news is bad news. The executive may have decided early on that the system is not worth using. If there are problems, you want to know about them before they get out of hand.

What do you need to know in order to use an executive information system effectively? First, how to access the system. There are several different methods, described in the checklist below, and they all have their benefits and drawbacks. When you are tailoring the system to each executive user, it could be worthwhile exploring the different access methods with the user to find which he or she prefers (assuming, that is, that there are alternatives available within the software you have chosen).

CHECKLIST 6.1: Methods of accessing an executive information system

Keyboard.
Benefits: Highly flexible and allows the user to input detailed textual or numeric information.
Drawbacks: Few executives have keyboard skills. Operating a keyboard is seen as a low-status activity.
[Note: In some executive information systems, a keyboard can be displayed on the screen and activitated by one of the means below, but it is obviously much slower to use.]
Mouse.
Benefits: Increasingly familiar with executives. Easy to link into system.
Drawbacks: Requires eye-hand co-ordination which may not come naturally to all executives.
Touch screen.
Benefits: Probably the simplest way of accessing a system.
Drawbacks: Can create arm ache after extensive use. Makes the screen smudgy with finger marks.
Infra-red keypad.
Benefits: Same ease of use as touch screen, without the arm ache.
Drawbacks: Can be difficult to position cursor when sitting some distance from screen.
Voice.
Benefits: What could be more natural?
Drawbacks: Technology not really ready to make this feasible. [Only one known executive information system has ever tried it.]

Although all executive information software is designed with the aim of solving the same kinds of executive problems, each package is different in (often important) details. Even so, looked at from your point of view as a user, there are certain common features. Exploring these features gives you an idea of the kind of tasks you should be able to perform with your personal executive information system.

The first of these features is the review book or briefing book; – different suppliers have their own term for what is broadly the same concept. The purpose of the review book is to let you, as a user, build up a simple library of screens of commonly used information. The review book may replace a paper-bound briefing book used before the executive information system or it may consist of new information that you have not previously reviewed regularly. Whichever it is, it is a repository of the information you refer to most frequently. The review book will probably be designed so that you can easily navigate around its pages. For example, there may be a menu which helps you to navigate through commonly used pages and there will be on-screen buttons that allow you to move to the next page or the last page. (See screen shot 6.1.)

		ACTUALS			GROUP	
		TOTAL MARKET				

	April	May	June	July	August
Turnover	1396053	1487875	1471272	1488895	1858764
Labour Costs	335469	361559	355236	359416	450442
Material Costs	284268	305222	301604	305255	381251
Marketing Costs	322698	310916	331848	358336	442238
Expenses	92905	101459	102425	104329	126747
Fixed Assets	78610	86593	86528	88522	108701
Stocks	22080	18614	22937	34594	34809
Debtors	4455618	4442246	4510343	4582190	5636675
Creditors	862248	935013	915976	940203	1168341
Cost of Sales	942434	977697	988688	1023007	1273931
Gross Margin	453618	510178	482584	465888	584833
Operating Profit	360713	408718	380159	361560	458086
Working Capital	3616450	3525847	3617305	3676581	4503144
Capital Employed	3695060	3612440	3703833	3765102	4611845

EIS-EPiC	VIEW	TURN	STYLE	DESIGN	MORE	HELP	DONE	22 Apr 92 Wednesday
213/20007								08:27

6.1 *A typical executive information screen contains several ways of navigating to other screens*

Depending on the precise details of your system, you may have some of the review book pages overlaid with hot spots. When a figure is a hot spot, you can select it to drill-down to the next layer of information below it. Similarly, that layer of information, which will probably be shown on a separate screen, may also have hot spots, which allow you to drill-down to lower levels of data. (See screen shot 6.2.) The drill-down gives you another way of moving around the review book.

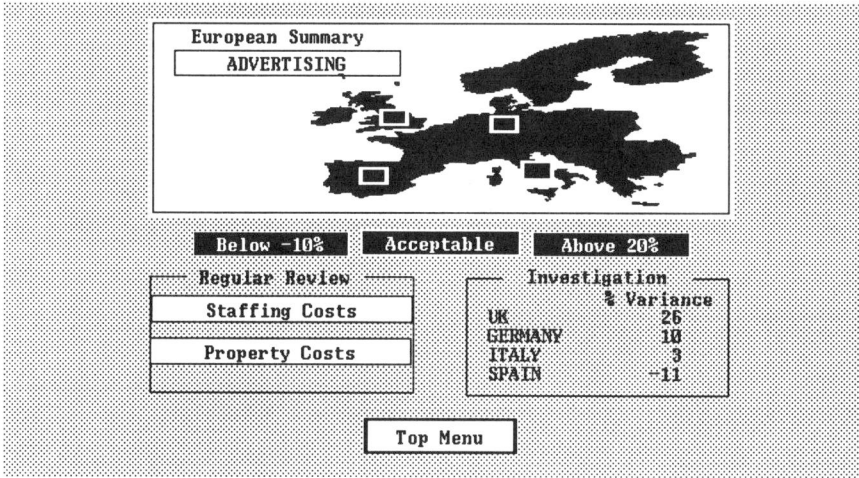

6.2 *A screen may have hot spots to let the user drill-down to lower levels of data*

In summary, then, you could have three main ways of moving about the review book – by menu, by next and last buttons, and by drill-down.

The second feature common to most executive information systems can best be described as an investigator. Again, details vary from one system to another, but the underlying concept allows you to access information intuitively from the underlying executive database to create two-dimensional or three-dimensional 'slices' of data. (See screen shot 6.3.) These will typically be slices which you cannot access as regular screens in the review book. The benefit of this is that it lets you look at the data in ways which were not possible before without a huge effort on the part of a data analyst. It lets you follow a hunch. The executive information system permits you to indulge your hunch in a few seconds and at practically no cost. In this way, you have time to gain more insights into how your business works than ever before.

The third feature is the ability to graph numeric information in a number of different ways. (See screen shot 6.4.) Again, graphing and charting features vary from one system to another but they will typically include line graphs, scatter graphs, bar charts,

Eclipse - [Model - [Untitled]]

File Edit Tools Actions Chart Options Table Font Window F1=Help

	C1	C2	C3	C4	C5	C6	C7
Q1							
Q2	ACTUALS						
Q3	GROUP						
Q4	TOTAL MARKET	April	May	June	July		
Q5	Labour Costs	335,468.61	361,558.99	355,235.65	359,416.09		
Q7	Marketing Costs	322,698.34	310,916.20	331,848.03	358,336.39		
R18							
R19							
R20							
Q6	SLICE 2						
Q8	GROUP						
Q9	TOTAL MARKET						
Q10	April	ACTUALS	BUDGET	FORECAST	HISTORY		
Q11	Turnover	396,052.66	434,970.59	300,505.76	334,115.32		
Q12	Labour Costs	335,468.61	349,065.23	369,121.94	325,430.53		
Q13	Material Costs	284,267.53	292,927.39	304,981.87	271,987.35		
Q14	Marketing Costs	322,698.34	316,076.51	334,012.46	296,573.99		
Q15	Expenses	92,905.10	90,046.95	94,596.32	82,602.71		
Q16	Fixed Assets	78,610.29	74,766.90	84,640.52	69,800.43		
Q17	Stocks	22,079.60	22,129.47	22,156.47	20,688.54		
R21							
R22							
R23							
R24							
R25							

6.3   *A user can call up a two-dimensional slice of data on to the screen*

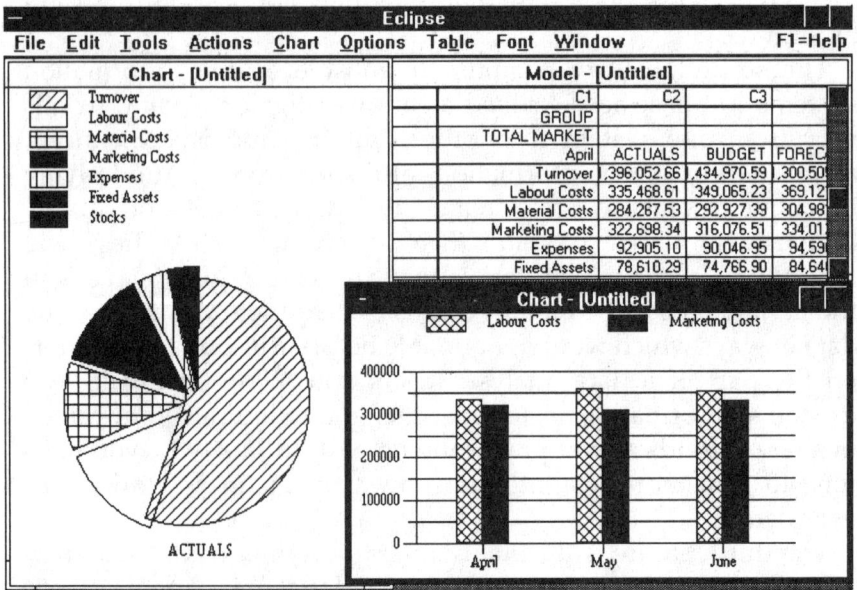

Eclipse

File Edit Tools Actions Chart Options Table Font Window F1=Help

Chart - [Untitled]

- Turnover
- Labour Costs
- Material Costs
- Marketing Costs
- Expenses
- Fixed Assets
- Stocks

ACTUALS

Model - [Untitled]

	C1	C2	C3
	GROUP		
	TOTAL MARKET		
April	ACTUALS	BUDGET	FOREC
Turnover	396,052.66	434,970.59	300,50
Labour Costs	335,468.61	349,065.23	369,12
Material Costs	284,267.53	292,927.39	304,98
Marketing Costs	322,698.34	316,076.51	334,01
Expenses	92,905.10	90,046.95	94,59
Fixed Assets	78,610.29	74,766.90	84,64

Chart - [Untitled]

Labour Costs   Marketing Costs

(bar chart: April, May, June; scale 0 to 400000)

6.4   *It is possible to graph numeric information in a number of different ways*

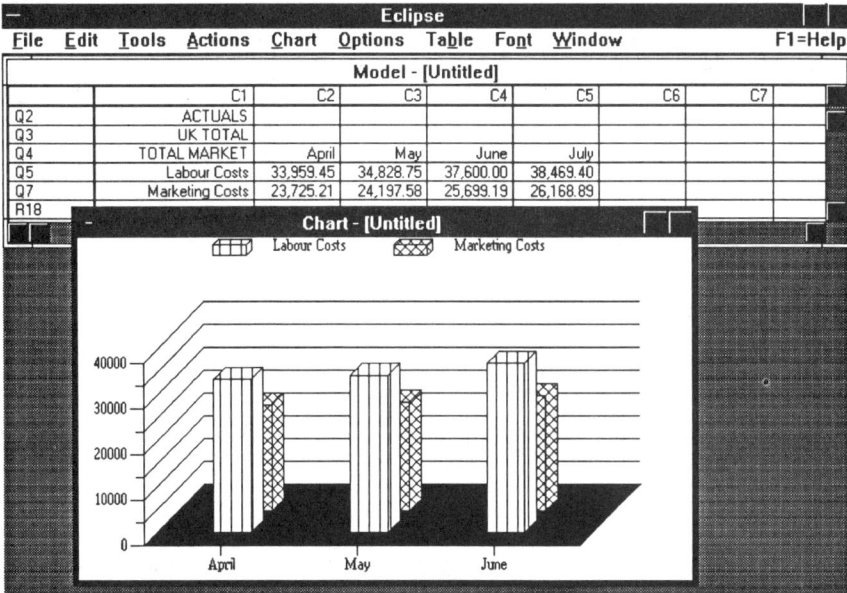

		C1	C2	C3	C4	C5	C6	C7
Q2		ACTUALS						
Q3		UK TOTAL						
Q4		TOTAL MARKET	April	May	June	July		
Q5		Labour Costs	33,959.45	34,828.75	37,600.00	38,469.40		
Q7		Marketing Costs	23,725.21	24,197.58	25,699.19	26,168.89		
R18								

6.5   Some executive information systems can create three-dimensional charts

line charts and pie charts. Within the charting facility, you will typically have a choice of solid, outlines or patterns. You may also be able to create three dimensional charts. (See screen shot 6.5.) The whole area of graphing and charting contains its own mysteries and it can pay to buy in some professional advice to get you started in this area. You need to be aware that a graph can mislead as easily as it can inform – for example, by adopting inappropriate scaling – and you need to make sure that the graphs and charts used in your executive information system add to rather than detract from the understanding of the information you are examining. Typically, you will be able to change numeric information into graphs and charts by accessing simple on-screen commands. (See screen shot 6.6.)

The fourth feature common to most executive information systems is the help screen. If you need to use help screens too often, the system has been badly designed. Even so, all users need extra help from time to time and this is often available by touching a help button always shown on the screen. The help should be 'context sensitive'. That means when you press the button, the help screen you are shown is relevant to the screen of

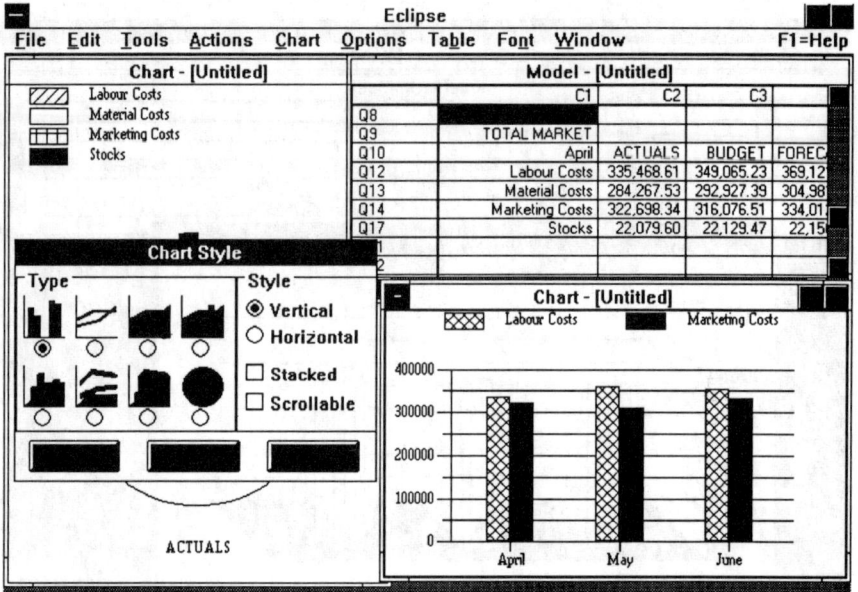

6.6 *Numeric information can be changed into graphs or charts through simple on-screen commands*

information you were looking at (and, possibly, the function you were trying to perform) when you selected it.

With all these and other features in the executive information system, you need to be able to use them easily, even intuitively. Above all, the designer needs to have created the system in such a way that the technology does not get in the way. In other words, as the user you do not need to know how the system works – just that it does. Using the system should hold no more fears than driving a car.

A Day's Work with an Executive Information System

As a reasonably experienced user of an executive information system, how might it help in your daily toil? You arrive at the office and one of your first tasks is to input your password which brings the system on-line. This is a simple process, for any executive information system worth its salt is designed to let you start work without the laborious log-on routines which take so much time on other computers.

110

Your first task is to use your executive information system to find out what's been happening since you went home last night. You might, for example, want an update on the trading position on the New York and Tokyo stock exchanges, or on certain selected shares. The system can deliver that information, downloaded automatically from external databases. You might want overnight financial or sales figures from overseas subsidiaries. These, too, can be downloaded to your system through communications links. You know you need to keep up with the business press and the trade and technical press that serves your market sectors, but you simply don't have time to read everything. The system 'reads' the publications you ask it to, using keyword selections to pick out stories that you might want to review personally on your screen. The screen lists them, the source of the story and the number of words in it.

During the day a Reuters/Press Association feed into your system can keep you up to date with the main facts of any breaking story you might need to know about fast. The system can be programmed to produce an on-screen alert if a story is fed into its memory containing a keyword or selection of keywords. The screen will warn you of the story's arrival, even if you are working on another task, or even if the system is not currently being used (providing it is still switched on).

Your early morning review of the overnight situation has thrown up a number of issues that you want to pursue or on which you would like more information. Using a 'clip and send' routine you mark out those portions of the screen containing information you want looked into. Then you send it, over the system's communication network, to the manager you want to investigate it. Perhaps you attach a semi-standard message that the system provides from a list such as 'What's this all about?' or 'More detail on these figures please.' The system automatically records which managers have received early morning missives from you. It will also record when their replies arrive. So, at any time, you can look into a file on your screen and see who you have asked for what information and who hasn't provided it.

That is the early morning review dealt with. Next, you need to see what lies ahead for the rest of the day. Although it is arguable whether office automation-type software, such as a diary, is really part of an executive information system, some systems include such facilities as a way of adding value to the total application. You call your diary on-screen and get an immediate list of today's appointments together with other important tasks for the day and information to watch out for. (The system reminds you that a competitor is announcing its annual results this morning. You make a note to call up the results on your screen later in the day and review them.)

Meanwhile, your diary has highlighted another problem. Your overnight review revealed some problems at the Australian subsidiary. You will need to spend time this morning sorting it out, which means re-scheduling a pre-arranged meeting with three other people. Fortunately, the other three are also on the executive information system and you operate an open diary system for office appointments. You can call all three diaries on to your screen simultaneously to find the first available time when all four of you can meet. In two days' time. Not too bad. You call up your file of semi-standard messages and send a notice of the new meeting time to all of them. The new meeting time will automatically appear as a provisional entry in their diaries.

That, probably, will be enough time at your screen for the moment. Few senior executives will spend more than an average of an hour a day using the system. But time is not the point – it is the quality of use and the value you get out of it that counts. You return to the system later in the morning. First, you want to review that competitor's results. For starters, you call up the Press Association story on the results which provides the basic figures and some background facts and comment.

Interesting, but you need to look at those results from your perspective. Perhaps you want to compare your competitors performance on certain key indicators against your own.

Easy. You can call up detailed performance data about listed companies from a number of on-line databases. Then you can use your system to build ratios from the raw data using simple menu commands. Perhaps you want to compare sales per employee, or profit per unit of capital employed or any one of literally thousands of commonly used business ratios. Then you can graph those ratios for the last few years. Revealing. They display some interesting trends in your competitor's business. How does that compare with your business? You create the same ratios out of your own performance data. Next graph the ratios over time on the same scale as your competitor. Then you superimpose one graph on top of the other. That's interesting. You'd not noticed that trend before. You file the screens away so that they can be called back automatically. You want to discuss this information at the next executive committee meeting.

Of course, you have been able to perform this kind of analysis in the past; but it always took so long. You had analysts beavering away in a back room poring over annual reports and wielding coloured pens and graph paper. By the time you got the graphs, you'd forgotten why you originally asked for them. In any event, your mind was now focused on a new problem. One of the big benefits of the executive information system, you've noticed, is that you get the information at the time you want to examine the problem.

You plan to discuss this problem at the executive committee this afternoon. That would never have been possible before because the information simply would not have been ready in time. Now, as you enter the boardroom, you know that the information you want to make your case will be available on the executive information system. When you first got the system, you thought its only value would be to provide you with information. You didn't realise that one of its strongest benefits is to provide information to help you persuade colleagues to pursue policies you believe are necessary. Now the information displays you saved this morning are going to be called up on the presentation screen in the boardroom to help you make your case.

Another thing: you seem to remember that a lot of time at executive committee meetings used to be spent arguing about who had the correct information. You don't do that now because you all share the same executive database. There is, as that pompous bore from the IT department put it, 'the same version of the corporate truth'. Well, at least all the numbers agree.

There is no doubt that you have immediate attention when you call your graphs up on to the boardroom screen. You've never considered yourself too bad at putting a case – after all, a lot of senior executive's time is spent in that activity – but you have to admit it is much easier when you can show them what you mean. What did that proverb say? 'A picture is worth a thousand words'. It can certainly save a thousand words – and more – of talking, because what you mean is as clear as, well, a picture. Besides, everybody seems to understand what you mean better. There are not so many questions designed to draw out your meaning. Instead, there is a better quality discussion about the problem and what should be done about it.

Here, again, you know the executive information system is going to come into play. There will initially be as many suggestions for action as people sitting round the table. Some of the suggestions may sound reasonable, others more far-fetched. You can use the modelling facilities in the executive information system to game-plan the effects of all of them if you want to. That finds out exactly what might happen and, this afternoon, it reveals that one of the more far-fetched suggestions is not so wide of the mark after all. You would almost certainly never have got to that idea without the executive information system because the unlikely idea would have involved too much work to investigate in detail.

You arrive at some decisions after what has, since you installed the executive information system, become a typical well informed and productive discussion. There is some action you need to take before you leave tonight. Back in your office, your executive information system will provide some more information you need and you communicate with those managers, some overseas, who need to take action. Their replies will be waiting for you when you switch on the executive information system tomorrow morning.

The Impact on the Organisation

Using an executive information system is likely to have an impact at two levels. The first, as we have seen, is on your daily working life as a manager. The second is on the processes and structure of your organisation. By now, it should be plain that an executive information system is not just about introducing a neat and useful piece of new technology. It is about beginning fundamental reform of the management process which, in turn, may lead to a changed corporate structure. When you first introduce an executive information system, the impact on management processes may not seem too fundamental. There is a limit to the amount of impact a small system, used by a tiny cadre of executives, will have. However as the executive information system spreads through the organisation, the impact will accelerate exponentially.

This means that when you start to introduce an executive information system you need to be aware that you have started a process of change that will have far-reaching consequences.

Indeed, much of the business benefit from the system comes from its ability to help you change outdated processes and structures. Even so, unless you are prepared for the strategic decisions this will involve, you will not be well placed to gain the really big prizes that executive information systems can deliver.

So just what kind of impact on your organisation can you expect a growing executive information system to have?

More timely reporting. Month-end financial reports – the kind of data that normally used to be in the briefing book – should be delivered more quickly. This, in itself, means you will be taking decisions on information which is more relevant. You will also be able to take corrective action for problems revealed in month-end financials more swiftly. In fact, you may find that the executive information system will reduce the importance of the month-end briefing book by making information available continuously. This, in turn, could change the way you review performance and take decisions about future plans.

EXAMPLE: Transport Development Group

Transport Development Group (TDG) is the parent company of about 60 operating companies in the UK, mainland Europe, the US and Australia. The company is managed through eight divisional offices and its companies are based in eight different countries each with their own currency. TDG installed an executive information system to collect and consolidate information on weekly, monthly and annual timescales. The system consolidates company information in different currencies through divisions to the centre so that executives can view the information across divisions, companies and currencies in almost any combination. The monthly model which is the main source of management information consists of quite detailed profit and loss accounts and balance sheets together with summaries of authorised and incurred capital expenditure and source and use of funds. Executives can view the information in its local currency, divisional reporting currency, and sterling.

Reduces bureaucracy. The executive information system removes the need for a great deal of paper-based reporting, both of financial and non-financial data. Even so, some companies maintain their paper reports even though information is available on the executive information system. In these cases, the paper report is the management equivalent of the comfort blanket. When the managers grow up and learn to trust their executive information system, they will not need the paper reports any more. Apart from the reduction in paper and printing bills, the executive information creates an opportunity to save on the bureaucratic machinery needed to create and store them.

Increases executive span of control. Management academics have written a lot of theory about the optimum span of control of an average manager. The executive information system means they will have to revise their views. The main constraint in the past on increasing your span of control has been the amount of reporting information you need to review from individual operating units you control. The executive information system can remove that block to a wider span. This is especially true if you are controlling operating units which have a similar internal structure and method of operation and where your 'mental model' of the critical success factors of the units is similar for all of them.

As a result of increasing the span of control for senior managers, the executive information system provides an opportunity to create a flatter organisational structure. Although there are not too many cases where this has happened so far, there are some examples. It is an issue that some experienced users of executive information systems are now looking at much more closely. Plainly, if you can increase your span of control, the need for some of the intermediate layers of management may be removed. That will also reduce bureaucracy, because at least some of the work of intermediate layers of management involves passing information up the management hierarchy and decisions down.

More customer-responsive. Creating a flatter organisation should make your company more responsive to customer needs. There are fewer layers of management between the customer and the top of the company. This means information about customer needs can reach the top faster. Similarly, you can use the executive information system to monitor customer needs directly. For possibly the first time, the executive information system gives you the chance to develop a set of critical success factors and key performance indicators directly related to serving customer needs, and to collect the information you need to monitor them regularly, in a cost-effective and non-bureaucratic way.

Makes restructuring easier. In a sense, creating a flatter organisational structure is a form of corporate restructuring. However there are other ways in which your executive information system can help. The business climate is one in which acquisitions, mergers and divestments take place more regularly than ever. An executive information system's modelling features provide an ideal framework in which to game-plan the effect of any corporate change on key performance variables such as profit, capital employed or price-earnings ratio. Moreover, the discipline on information structures, which developing and using an executive information system imposes, means that separate units of the business can be hived off or moved to different divisions with clinical efficiency.

7

LEARNING FROM OTHERS' EXPERIENCE

'Learning without thought is labour lost; thought without learning is perilous.'

– Confucius, *Analects*

Tales from the Front Line

It is possible to gain value from using an executive information system, no matter what your specific job function. Having said that, the bulk of users of the systems fall into a number of categories. These are (1) chairmen, chief executives and managing directors; (2) financial directors and financial controllers; (3) sales and marketing management; (4) subsidiary or divisional managing directors or general managers and (5) management support professionals, often business analysts of one flavour or another or information systems people involved in developing executive information systems. Depending on your job function, you will use your system with a specific focus. You can get some ideas about the best way to use the system both by considering some general principles and by looking at the path-finding experiences of other users.

Managing directors. Executive information systems are probably the first computer system to provide facilities that are directly relevant to the working lives of chairmen, chief executives and managing directors. Management theorists like to draw a distinction between the roles of the chairman on the one hand and managing director on the other. According to this theory, the task of the chairman is to look outwards, to develop strategy and

119

position the company in the light of market and economic changes. The role of the managing director is to look inwards to ensure that the company has the optimum corporate structure to deliver its products and services and the most efficient staffing and facilities to do so.

Unlike other computer systems, the executive information system is ideally suited to delivering the kind of external data that the chairman might want to review. Similarly, the system can provide better quality reporting data to enable the managing director to gauge the operational profitability and efficiency of individual operating units. In the past, this top echelon of managers has usually received its information carefully sifted and moulded by business analysts. The advantage is that the MD can focus on a limited amount of digestible information which is presented to highlight trends and key developments. The draw-back is that it can make him or her reliant on the corporate view of business analysts. He or she only sees the information considered important; and moreover, sees it through their eyes. Several chairmen and chief executives have said that one of the great benefits they have discovered from using an executive informa-tion system is the ability to free themselves from a particular corporate view, to delve more deeply into source data themselv-es, perhaps to browse through data they would not normally see, and develop their own view of what is important and how it should be interpreted.

EXAMPLE: The knights of executive information systems

There is a growing roll-call of executive information system users at the top of major companies. They include Sir Denys Henderson, chairman of ICI; Sir Bryan Nicholson, chairman of the Post Office and Sir Colin Marshall, deputy chairman and chief executive of British Airways. (You don't need a knigh-thood, however, to use an executive information system!) Sir Denys Henderson uses his system at a strategic level to review the operating performance of ICI in relation to its competitors. He can also use his system to review the effects of acquisitions, mergers or divestments. Other chief execut-ives can use their systems to review the performance of competitors against their own. They have access to external information, including competitors, brokers' reports, economic indicators, industry news, general news, stock exchange data

---

and currency. Sir Bryan Nicholson and other members of the Post Office Board use their system to review key features of the performance of the five businesses within the Post Office Corporation. Within the Royal Mail, one of the five main business of the Post Office, the managing director is able to review a district performance report on his executive information system. The system shows the financial performance of each of the 65 districts (aggregated into five territories) against budget with variance analysis. The system also contains an 'executive alert' which highlights poor performance which can then be investigated using drill-down techniques. At British Airways, Sir Colin Marshall – who sometimes gets an assistant to use the system – can review future operating scenarios with his system.

CHECKLIST 7.1: Applications for chief executives

- Monitoring division and subsidiary results
- Driving corporate-wide strategic programmes (i.e. total quality programmes)
- Monitoring takeover targets/threats
- Reviewing macroeconomic data
- Receiving selected news items
- Game-planning future business strategies

Financial executives. Typically, the financial director or financial controller will have had more experience of using computers than the managing director. (In quite a few companies, the financial director has taken board level responsibility for information technology.) Most financial directors and financial controllers will be used to receiving computer generated reports and many will be familiar with using spreadsheets. Thus one of the main interests for this management function is gaining access to financial information more flexibly and in a more timely fashion than before. Another interest is in the ability to add value to the data in a way that is not possible (or, at least, very difficult) when using a spreadsheet.

Like managing directors, financial directors also have an interest in some external data, especially relevant share price move-

ments, currency fluctuations, (possibly) commodity price movements and some macroeconomic data for business planning and
developing budget assumptions. Again, an executive information
system makes it possible for a financial director to access much of
this information directly, rather than through middle managers.
Financial directors have found executive information systems
particularly valuable for reviewing monthly results of divisions or
subsidiaries against budget, using variance reporting to highlight
problem areas. Drill-down facilities provide a means of obtaining
lower level data that would previously have meant a special
request and perhaps a long delay or which would simply not have
been available.

Financial controllers have found that executive information
systems are well suited as a means of delivering the information
needed to monitor and control the treasury function. Using
information from external data feeds, it is possible to have data
such as currency exchange rates and different money market rates
monitored continuously. Even more usefully, the executive information system can be used to perform trend analysis on such
data. Some companies have already developed their own highly
sophisticated algorithms for performing that task. Two senior
finance managers between them demonstrate some of the applications and benefits an executive information system can deliver
at this level.

EXAMPLE: Ciba Geigy UK

Brian Kerr, finance director of Ciba Geigy UK uses his system
to obtain updates on key financial and performance measures.
The system provides him with information such as sales or
productivity performance, new capital investment and group
head count. For treasury use, the system provides information
about levels and costs of borrowings and foreign exchange
activity. According to Kerr, the main benefit is the ability to use
one consistent database of figures, much less paperwork and
information selectivity.

EXAMPLE: Simon Engineering

Barry Finan, a divisional finance director at Simon Engineering, has speeded up the month-end reporting of companies in
his division with an executive information system. Reports are
fed down telephone lines to Finan's computer which performs

currency conversions and consolidates the figures. Then the system generates the key ratios used to monitor the business.

CHECKLIST 7.2: Financial executives' applications

- Developing and testing budget scenarios
- Monitoring results against budget
- Monitoring FX, money market, etc. rates and movements
- Controlling cash flow
- Producing key ratios

Sales and marketing executives. Computers have played their part in marketing and sales operations for years, but most often at the transaction level – where individual sales take place – or at middle management level. In the retail industry, the last few years have seen growing interest in using the data collected by electronic point of sale systems for marketing and sales management purposes. Yet the use of computer systems by sales or marketing directors or other senior executives in major companies was rare until executive information systems appeared.

Essentially, the executive information system has the power to do to sales data for marketing management what it does to finance data for financial management. The same value added facilities such as graphing and charting can be used on sales data. Sales and marketing executives can use features such as exception reporting to view sales figures by region, salesperson or product line. In this way, it is possible to highlight poorly performing areas for special attention. Moreover, depending on the complexity of the system, it may be possible to drill-down to lower levels to find out the reasons for poor sales performance. Used creatively, the executive information system becomes more than just a reporting tool. The system can, for example, produce data about comparative brand performance which can then be used by sales people to win larger orders, more shelf space or competitive brand replacement.

EXAMPLE: Courage Take Home Trade
Courage Take Home Trade, the off-licence subsidiary of the brewer, uses an executive information system to monitor sales of its leading brands such as Kronenburg, Hofmeister and

---

Miller Lite. Managers use the system to drill-down to sales detail and uncover previously unobserved facts about brand and store performance. The system has also improved presentation materials so that managers are better prepared when meeting important customers. Courage believes the system has helped to boost its market position from sixth to a claimed second place in the take-home market.

CHECKLIST 7.3: Sales and marketing applications

- Developing sales targets
- Monitoring actual sales against sales targets
- Producing comparative brand performance data
- Monitoring comparative advertisement spending data
- Testing impact of marketing campaigns
- Game-planning new product launches

Subsidiary or divisional senior executives. One of the effects of introducing an executive information system at the top of a corporation is to make the activities of subsidiaries or divisions more transparent or visible to executives at corporate level. This, in turn, has often prompted senior divisional or subsidiary executives to want to find out more about their own organisation. In a positive sense, corporate level management has set an example and shown them the way. In a more negative sense, the subsidiary management has recognised the potential difficulties of having inadequate or late information to present to corporate level or of knowing less about some aspects of their operation than corporate executives.

In many cases, a subsidiary or divisional executive information system will be a baby version of the corporate system. However whereas the corporate system will, of its nature, tend to focus on strategic issues, the subsidiary system will look more at operational and tactical questions. Curiously, many subsidiaries that develop executive information systems after their corporate management choose not to use the same software as their chiefs. There may be an element of politics in asserting their independence; but, also, very few subsidiary executive information systems seem to have direct network links to the corporate-level

124

system. Again, there may be an element of politics in this in keeping tighter control over the 'ownership' of the subsidiary's own data. Even so, a subsidiary executive information system can be of great value not only in controlling operations, but in developing data to present at corporate level.

EXAMPLE: British Steel Distribution

British Steel Distribution (BSD), a wholly-owned subsidiary of British Steel, uses the presentation features of its system to provide operating data to its parent in a professional and organised way. Senior BSD managers can use graphs and charts to reveal trends that corporate level executives may not have known about. In that way, British Steel executives become more realistically aware of the problems and opportunities of BSD.

CHECKLIST 7.4: Subsidiary's applications

- Collecting and monitoring operational data
- Developing divisional business plans
- Presenting results to corporate level management
- Providing data to defend or bid for budgets

Management support professionals. The management support professionals who have most to do with executive information systems tend to fall into two categories. First, there are the business analysts who sift and interpret data for their bosses; providing reports, briefing books, and other management information. Then there are the information systems staff, skilled in writing software and developing applications, who are called on to carry out the more technical aspects of installing an executive information system, such as building the screens or setting up the network.

In some cases, an executive information system has displaced business analysts. In others, some business analysts continue to thrive, plying their arcane trade with the aid of the executive information system. Not all companies that install a system decide to abolish the traditional monthly hard-copy briefing book. Indeed, there is no reason why they should if they find the briefing book comforting or useful. Where users retain an existing report, however, it is important that business analysts should help them to get some added value from the system. Otherwise they ask the question: 'What extra value does this give us?'

Information systems staff will use the application building tools to develop new applications. Some executive information system software suppliers like to claim that their software is so easy to use that executives can build their own applications. There are cases of senior executives becoming enthusiasts for the technology and building applications. But in 19 cases out of 20 this will not happen. The information systems professional will be expected to build the applications and handle all the other issues, such as data collection and interfacing with other computers, to ensure the executive information system runs smoothly. In doing this, he or she may need access to the range of system building tools which should be included in the system building toolkit. Features that might be needed include a fourth generation-type language, screen painter, menu builder, report writer, communications control language and data import/extract editors.

CHECKLIST 7.5: Management support professionals' applications

- Building briefing books with added value
- Adding value to existing applications
- Developing new applications

Using Executive Information Systems in Different Businesses

Executive information systems have possible applications in most organisations in the private and public sector. Their use is not restricted by the activities or functions of the organisation. Thus, systems are already installed and delivering useful benefits in organisations as diverse as supermarket chains and government departments. In the early days, when the executive information system market was dominated by mainframe software, only the largest organisations – mostly Times 500 companies – installed systems, if only because their cost was considerable. With the widespread adoption of PC-based systems, much smaller organisations can benefit. A few years ago, it was suggested that £50 million turnover might be a useful benchmark as the entry point for an executive information system user. Today, that entry point has dropped considerably to the upper single figure millions.

The applications that users will perform in different organisations will overlap – for example, monitoring financial performance against budgets is common to most organisations. Consultant Robert Bittlestone[1] has produced a list of executive information system application areas common to most lines of business (checklist 7.6).

CHECKLIST 7.6: Application areas for most organisations

- Acquisition analysis
- Bank line renegotiation
- Bid defence team
- Broker presentation
- Cash-flow monitoring
- Competitor evaluation
- Cost driver exercise
- Gross margin improvement
- Manpower reduction
- Market segment analysis
- Overhead reduction
- Post-capex review
- Redesigned board report
- Service level monitoring
- Shareholder value analysis
- Strategic plan creation
- Subsidiary budget review
- Working capital control
- Year-end forecast review

Apart from these and other possible application areas with wide application, different kinds of organisations are already developing their own tailored and, in some cases, unique applications to meet the challenges they face.

Manufacturing. Global forces at work make manufacturing a more hazardous activity than ever before. A decade or so ago, manufacturing a specific product was regarded as a specialised activity. Today, the act of manufacturing itself is increasingly seen as the specialised activity, irrespective of the end product. As a result, we are seeing the beginning of a major shift in the world balance of manufacturing power, increasingly to the Pacific Rim and third world countries. In this climate, the careful control of inputs, such as materials, labour and overheads, as well as of margins, is critical. So is the question of quality; quality is rapidly becoming the driving force of manufacturing success.

In this climate, an executive information system has many possible roles to play. At MK Electric, a maker and supplier of electrical products, a system delivers daily production, sales and order information to senior managers three hours earlier than before. At GPT, the joint GEC-Plessey company that makes the System X telephone exchange, a system is used to consolidate vital manufacturing information for a fortnightly directors' briefing.

CHECKLIST 7.7: Manufacturing applications

- Planning manufacturing schedules
- Monitoring and trending raw material prices
- Driving total quality management programmes
- Controlling and accessing manufacturing documentation
- Monitoring production, order and sales data

FMCG. In the fast moving consumer goods market, business problems are becoming more intractable and difficult to solve. In the battle for store shelf space and customer pounds, strong branding and product differentiation have become even more vital issues. Increasingly, long term success is founded on an ability to identify the different customer appeal factors in a product and build on their strengths. Doing this often means detecting patterns and trends buried in a mass of indigestible statistics. Trying to perform that kind of task in the past has meant hours, possibly days or weeks, of painstaking work as different hypotheses are tested. It is a task for which an executive information system, supported by a powerful modelling capability, could have been invented. A marketing or brand manager can slice and dice a mass of sales and market data to discover patterns that would otherwise remain undetected.

Similarly, anticipating market needs is becoming a more difficult task as markets tend to fragment and develop their own concerns and dynamics. This makes product positioning a more difficult task. One product may need to be fine-tuned to make it acceptable to several different market-places. Again, an executive information system provides an ideal way of slicing and dicing market research data to uncover patterns that guide marketing executives to more reliable decisions.

Where used, an executive information system has aided FMCG companies. At UB Brands, a United Biscuits company, the executive information system revealed that the company had lost market share in one segment during a Christmas period despite an overall rise in sales. Marketing managers were able to take action to correct the problem.

CHECKLIST 7.8: FMCG applications

- Analysing product sales data
- Analysing market research data
- Driving market positioning and branding strategy
- Managing customer service programmes
- Competitor brand monitoring

Financial services. In the financial services market liberalisation greatly increased competition; but companies initially rode this during the boom years of the middle eighties when there seemed to be plenty of business for everyone. As the market for financial services has become tougher, the truth about increased competition has finally come home to roost. As with FMCG, the market for financial services has fragmented, making the task of identifying targets and product differentiation more difficult. And with many financial services products – mortgages or building society and bank deposit accounts, for example – the competitive edge comes from a small adjustment at the margin. Yet that marginal adjustment can make the difference between profit or loss.

In this climate, financial services providers are looking to control costs more tightly than ever before. They are also seeking new marketing opportunities more actively and developing new products more quickly than before. They also need to react to volatile market conditions – such as changes in interest rates – more speedily. Moreover, in planning for the future, for instance assessing the likely demand for new products, interpreting and understanding macroeconomic trend data is increasingly important. In all of these areas, financial services providers, including banks, building societies, insurance companies and others, are already finding executive information systems a valuable tool.

At Royal Insurance, for example, an executive information system provides details on a number of business performance measures including quarterly results, profit before tax, head office expenses and world staffing levels. At the Woolwich Building Society, a system helps managers review information about lending, investments, financial performance and competitor results.

CHECKLIST 7.9: Financial services applications
- Analysing market research data
- Trending macroeconomic data
- Monitoring product performance
- Reviewing and controlling account performance
- Game-planning new product performance

Retailing. Retail is detail – a truth about the business which has become even more obvious in recent years. As profit margins are squeezed, the task of controlling all costs – staffing, buildings, overheads, marketing – becomes more urgent. At the same time, retailers have become more aware of ways in which sales can be increased by fine adjustments to prices and by special offers campaigns. Yet carrying out such a programme of activity, monitoring its effect and maintaining profit margins, requires even more information.

With the pattern of retailing changing more dramatically than at any period in British shopping history, retailers face a new range of crucial decisions about future investment plans. They are decisions which involve the compilation, analysis and understanding of unprecedented amounts of information. Eastern Electricity, for example, uses its system to analyse weekly sales data from the shops in its region. Managers can slice and dice the data to examine sales by product or by shop or a combination of both. Using this information, they gain a better idea of product sales opportunities.

CHECKLIST 7.10: Retailing applications
- Analysing demographic data for planned or existing stores
- Game-planning different product mixes for stores
- Monitoring sales by store or product line
- Controlling costs and overheads

Utilities. Companies in this sector, including electricity, water and gas, have been privatised and exposed to harsher market disciplines in the last decade. As a result, these are frequently companies that are undergoing far-reaching change programmes and that are adopting new cultures as part of the change. It is often the case that an executive information system is used by a company undergoing dramatic change and the utilities are no exception. In a typical pattern, the utility acquired its system a few months before or after it became privatised. Then it started to monitor a range of customer service indicators as well as traditional financial performance data. The ability to measure customer performance has often been an important driver in the utilities' ability to develop a customer service culture.

Another factor for suppliers in businesses such as electricity, gas and water is the need to provide information to industry regulators as well as government departments. Some businesses, such as water, are under tougher 'green' pressures to protect the environment. In some instances, information from executive information systems helps to drive these programmes. For example, at Wessex Water, managers can access a system to gain key information about supply problems and the time taken to fix them, as well as obvious customer service measures such as the amount of time taken to answer the phone.

131

CHECKLIST 7.11: Utilities' applications

- Driving customer service programmes
- Monitoring environmental improvement programmes
- Controlling capital investment
- Consolidating data for reports to regulatory bodies

Public authorities. Although public authorities have adopted executive information systems more quietly than some organisations in the private sector, there is a wide range of applications, especially in the health service. In the NHS the widespread adoption of systems is largely driven by the need to control costs as funding comes under tighter constraints. For example, at the South Lincolnshire Health Authority, a system has become the 'cornerstone' of a resources management programme. One hospital in the area has created models for each of its eight speciality areas (such as general medicine or gynaecology) and another for all of them. Users can review information about clinical activity and the doctors to whom the activity relates.

Outside the NHS, other public sector executive information system users include government departments such as Social Security, Employment and the Foreign Office and agencies such as the Post Office. Even the military are now interested in the use of executive information systems. RAF Strike Command, for example, has built a system to monitor the performance of its aircraft in its groups and squadrons.

CHECKLIST 7.12: Public sector applications

- Reviewing service activity and delivery
- Monitoring implementation of policy objectives
- Controlling capital expenditure programmes

8

LOOKING TO THE FUTURE

'Future shock . . . is the consequence of having to make too many decisions about too many new and unfamiliar problems in too short a time. We are in collision with tomorrow.'

— Alvin Toffler, *The Observer*

The Biggest Challenge

Executive information systems can help to manage the business of today; but can they manage the business of tomorrow? This, in a sense, is the biggest challenge for these systems. For business success in the next decade will depend on the degree to which the corporation can manage change. Yet, in a changing business world, are there any fixed points of reference? Very few. Professor Charles Handy of the London Business School suggests any self-respecting company of today will have quadrupled its turnover in real terms in the last ten years and halved its core staff.[1] Although some famous corporate names can match up to the first part of that equation, not so many have achieved the second part. Yet Handy's benchmark is a measure of what the global enterprise should have achieved in order to remain an international front runner in its market-places.

The challenge for the next ten years is not much less. This means that today's corporation faces a simple choice – change or die. The role of the executive information system in all this should not be overstated. It cannot replace the mission, the vision, the purpose which a business needs in order to accomplish its goals.

An executive information system is a business tool, not a magic potion.

Yet the role of the executive information system should not be under-estimated either. The system may not be a potion, but it is a potent agent of change in the right management hands. As we have seen, it can provide the insight into the avalanche of facts that helps to make the incomprehensible understandable. It also provides a means of getting information quickly so that you can react to the unexpected. 'What we anticipate seldom occurs, what we least expect generally happens,' said Benjamin Disraeli. He was speaking of politics in the nineteenth century, but his words are even more true of business in the twentieth.

The executive information system, then, has a role in managing change, both expected and unexpected. We have already looked at many different kinds of applications for executive information systems. Some focus on historical review, such as those applications that compare out-turns with budgets or estimates. They help you to see where you have come from. But you also need to see where you are heading. Other applications, such as trend analysis and the use of macroeconomic data for forecasting, help you to plan for the future. Yet, useful as these are, they do not, by themselves, help you reach out towards the vision of the company you want to create in the future.

Can an executive information system help you do this? There is a danger that if you use executive information systems to replicate old-style methods of reporting, you will actually accelerate corporate decline rather than change for the future. You will be focused even more precisely on yesterday's problems. Instead, you need to see the executive information system as part of the change process itself, designed to accelerate your management focus on the future.

Further, you need to use the system to link strategy to day-to-day business activities and to make sure that those activities serve the vision. As part of the change process strategy needs to take centre stage in the daily life of the business and operations must be made the servant of it. It is quite possible to set strategic objectives – winning a certain percentage of market share in a given country, for example – and then use the executive information system to monitor how operations help to achieve the strategy. When you review operations on your executive information system, whether they be financials, production, sales or customer satisfaction figures, you need to review them not only against historical targets from your own company but against strategic objectives. Moreover, you need to monitor your own company's performance in many different areas, not only against internal targets but against standards set by competitors. For it is in that comparison that you will learn whether you are winning or losing the business battle. Again, that is a task an executive information system is especially well placed to perform.

EXAMPLE: Xerox Corporation

In the US, Xerox Corporation has built an executive information system specifically to support its strategic long-range planning process. Xerox's strategic planning office has introduced a standard five-page reporting document which is used by all of the company's 25 strategic business units. The document is delivered through the executive information system. The five screens of the document break down as follows:

1. Marketing strategy and performance, including a discussion of the mission, market, strategy and boundaries of the SBU.

2. Industry review looking at the business unit's strengths in terms of those critical success factors needed to gain or sustain competitive advantage.

3. A report from the SBU's general manager on the industry situation. Includes details of the major external uncertainties that could affect the business.

4. Financial and reporting data.

5. Senior management assessment of each strategic business unit's plans. On this page, plans are either signed off or rejected and requests for further information are made.

Information from this document – about actions, due dates and so on – is fed into other company databases so that its achievement can be monitored at an operational level.

New Application Areas

Until now, most executive information systems have concentrated on monitoring financial reporting data. It is not hard to find the reasons why. In most companies, monthly briefing books are still dominated by financial data. In some, about the only data that is actually computerised is financial. This means that executive information systems developers have had something of a Hobson's Choice when looking for data to include in an executive information system.

Yet among management thinkers and some successful companies, there is a growing realisation that monitoring a business solely with financial data is dangerous. As one management consultant says: 'It's like steering a ship by its wake.' One problem is that financial reports always look at historical information, the past rather than the future. The executive information system can partly tackle that problem by providing trend analysis. Yet that does not alter the fact that the business is still being run from a narrow information base. Indeed, the problem is thrown into a sharp spotlight by those companies that perform a rigorous exercise to identify their critical success factors. They find that many of the critical success factors are not measured in financial terms, but by other factors such as product quality, customer service and so on.

Most forward thinking companies are now coming round to the view that they need a much broader base of information to run the business. They need what management consultants Nolan Norton call a 'balanced scorecard'[2], a collection of measures that will help managers to create shareholder value in the future. According to the Nolan Norton Institute, those measures are:

- Financial: high level measures focused on the creation of shareholder value.
- Customer: measures on business performance from the customers' points of view.
- Process: the performance of key internal business processes in terms of quality, speed and productivity.
- Learning: the ability of the organisation to improve continuously and innovate in its products, services and processes.

No doubt different managers will argue about the precise balance you should strike between the different measures, but there is an emerging consensus that business needs to be able to measure – often for the first time – activities that have never been measured before. After all, as Tom Peters, the author of *Thriving on Chaos*[3], wrote: 'What gets measured, gets done.' All this brings the executive information system centre stage. In many cases, you will need to create new measurement processes to gather data for the balanced scorecard and you will need to provide senior executives with a tool for reviewing it.

In the next few years it is likely that we will see many more executive information system applications developed in new areas. These areas will include:

Global control. The problems of managing a modern business are multiplied by its global reach. Traditionally, the reporting processes of international businesses have been devalued, at least in part, by the extended timescales they take. By the time information reaches head office it might just as well be ancient history. In the future, effective global control will mean collecting and analysing information far more quickly, sometimes in 'real time'. (Also, as we have already seen, it will also mean collecting more than financial data.) An executive information system, linked by networks to databases in overseas operations, should be able to collect information more regularly and more swiftly than previous reporting systems.

Goal seeking. Many computer users are familiar with the technique of asking what-if? questions, a technique you can use in both executive information and other computer systems. Less familiar is the technique of goal seeking, which basically puts the what-if? technique into reverse. For example, if you have determined a particular level of profit you want to make, you can ask the system to calculate the level of sales needed to hit that target. The technique is especially valuable for testing the viability of business plans. Skilfully used, it can show you the bottlenecks – not enough sales people, perhaps – in achieving specific plans. The modelling and presentation techniques of an executive information system make it ideal for goal seeking applications.

Total quality management. The need for TQM programmes is now widely accepted in manufacturing industry and increasingly accepted in service industries, especially financial services. Yet the Achilles' Heel of such programmes is often the measurement process. Too often, the programmes are measured in terms of inputs – the number of staff who have been on training programmes, for example – rather than outputs, such as the number and type of rejects from a production line or customer complaints. In the future, more managers will use executive information systems to create a control environment for monitoring and measuring the impact of TQM programmes.

Cash flow. Most businesses have always included cash-flow forecasting among the financial reports. Yet, curiously, it has often been given less importance than other financials, such as profit margins or expenses. Furthermore, many large companies find it difficult to measure the cash flow of their component parts in any detail. But that is the kind of finely tuned information that you need if you are to find ways of improving overall cash flow. It is an application that executive information systems will increasingly be asked to perform. Indeed, it is an application that could deliver considerable value, especially to highly geared businesses facing recessionary cash-flow difficulties.

Shareholder value analysis: The idea of creating shareholder value is becoming more important in the management objectives of many companies. In the past, major corporations tended to engage specialist consultants to conduct *ad hoc* exercises to determine their shareholder value. Of course, like other figures in a dynamic company, shareholder value is constantly changing. Some companies are now developing shareholder value analysis applications in their executive information systems. The applications monitor shareholder value month by month, and by providing realistic up-to-date information help to keep this important issue before top executives.

Market-place performance. Increasingly, the success of a company in achieving its objectives is not measured by internal comparisons – beating last year's sales target, for example – but by comparisons with rivals. So market-place performance, to determine how the company is performing against competitors on such diverse measures as market share and return on capital employed, is more important. You can use your executive information system to collect comparative information from external databases. Graphs and charts can be used to provide screens that provide the results.

Performance-based compensation. There is a trend for more managers to receive a greater proportion of their compensation paid according to results. The problem is to determine what results to use and how to link them to the compensation package. Because the executive information system can be collecting a wide range of information – quality, customer satisfaction and so on – for other applications, you can use this data to build a performance package, which each manager can monitor on his or her own screen. Each package will be weighted in a different way, and the manager will be able to track his or her performance against the components of the package on screen as the reporting year progresses.

The applications above indicate just a few of the areas in which executive information systems will be increasingly used. Yet they represent just a tiny fraction of the different applications that organisations will run by the end of this decade. The executive information system may be just another management tool – albeit an important one – but like other management tools the winners will be those who use it with business creativity, imagination and flair.

New Technologies

Ten years ago, executive information systems as we know them today could not exist. The range of hardware, software and communications technologies needed to make them work simply did not exist. To make executive information systems a reality, developers needed powerful PCs or workstations with high definition colour screens, fourth generation languages, relational databases, graphical user interfaces, high-speed networks and other communications links and plenty more. Such technologies have helped to create the executive information systems of today.

Yet new technologies cascade into the world of information technology year by year. Some start life as a solution to an abstruse or technical problem; but, after time, these technologies are seen to have broader uses. Many of them will have applications in executive information systems in the years to come. Technologies worth keeping an eye on are:

Expert systems. These are based on the concept of artificial intelligence, first discussed by mathematicians as long ago as the 1930s. The first specialised expert systems appeared towards the end of the 1970s. Mostly, the technology is still used in niche areas such as insurance, where expert systems help policy administrators combine legal, financial and statistical data in policy writing. An expert system contains a language – often Prolog or Lisp – which is able to represent the facts in some area of human knowledge and an 'inference engine' which simulates the rules of logic that an experienced person would apply in taking decisions based on facts from the knowledge. Developers have already built expert systems that can make thousands of inferences on huge bodies of knowledge and present the human user with suggested decisions. Sometimes, expert systems are programmed to provide reasons for the decisions they suggest.

On the face of it, expert system techniques seem a natural idea to combine into executive information systems. The expert system could sift through raw data and provide suggested conclusions. In fact, while some manufacturers already claim to have incorporated expert systems into their executive information systems, the task is not straightforward. Expert systems work best when there are clear boundaries to the information they need to examine. This is often not the case with executive decisions which involve using 'soft' data from many sources and applying intuitive judgements which are not easily reduced to clear inference rules. Even so, as technical skills in this area develop, expert systems technology will find its way into executive information systems.

Object-oriented programmes: Or oops as they are more entertainingly called. Some, but not all, executive information systems are written using oops. In oops software both data and procedures are combined in software 'objects'. Similar objects are grouped into 'classes'. Data and procedures are 'inherited' through a class hierarchy. One of the benefits of the approach is that it can model complex problems. Another is that it helps developers build programmes which are fairly easy to maintain and change. It is likely that oops will be used increasingly in executive information systems.

Windows. This is the Microsoft operating system that provides a graphical front-end to user applications. Although not itself an executive information system, a number of suppliers have announced their intention to run their software under Windows. From the user's point of view, the big advantage of Windows is that it gives a consistent 'look and feel' to all applications, whether part of the executive information system or not. It can also interface with other Windows compliant applications. The downside is that applications run under Windows are more difficult to use, but this is probably an issue that Microsoft will tackle in future versions of the software.

For users who don't want to lose their current applications, Windows contains a special feature which lets users access more traditional MS-Dos (another operating system) applications in a less complicated way. Basically, the MS-Dos application is run from an icon controlled by Windows. There are plenty of other features in Windows – for example, a 'control panel' which lets users design their own look and feel to screens of information – which might encourage some developers to use the systems to develop executive-type applications. Even if that does not happen much, it is probable that Windows will become more important as an operating system platform for executive information system developers over the next three to five years.

Generally, Windows ought to be viewed as an emerging standard which the executive information systems developer will have to learn to harness. At the moment, the software looks more like a tool for 'power' workers, the IT professionals who develop executive information and other systems, rather than an ideal application platform for the senior level executive end-user.

Colour laptops. This could be a joker in the pack as far as executive information systems are concerned. The reasoning goes like this: the nature of executive work involves much travel from one place to another, so any really effective executive information system needs to move with the executive. Ergo: executives will increasingly use their executive information systems, either with a set of screens and sub-set of the executive database downloaded onto the laptop or through a communications link to the host computer. (Many laptops have built-in modems.) At the time of writing, colour laptops are extremely expensive – as much as £8,000 a unit – but like all new IT products, prices will eventually tumble.

Colour laser printers. Despite the increased use of executive information systems and other IT, talk of the 'paperless office' is still the nonsense it always was. According to some estimates, as much as 95 per cent of business information will still be presented on paper. Which makes the increased use of colour laser printers – like colour laptops, pricey but becoming less so – a good bet. Colour laser printers will be able to produce lustrous top quality management reports and presentation documents, often using screens of data created easily with the executive information system.

Cellular technology meets executive information systems. If voice communication can be transmitted to and from cars, why not data communication. A handful of managers already have laptop computers installed in their cars. It is not such a big step from that to providing some kind of automatic alert system that transmits urgent messages to managers on the move – or which allows them to call up data and work on it in the car.

Multimedia. At the moment, executive information systems mostly provide text and numbers as well as a range of graphs and charts. In the future, systems will increasingly include scanned images, colour pictures, videofilm and other images. There will also be sound, including voice-mail in which it will be possible for you to leave 'answering machine' type messages on other managers' workstations.

A Final Word

Are there any sure fire ways of making an executive information system a success?

None.

Are there any certain ways of dooming an executive information system to failure?

Plenty.

Does that mean introducing an executive information system is a high risk management activity?

Yes, but less than it used to be. There is now a growing body of good practice that the wise system developer can follow. This book has provided the details.

Given the risks, can a major organisation in the private or public sector afford to ignore executive information systems?

No. The tasks of managing organisations are becoming so much more complex, only those that harness information technology in creative and user-friendly ways will win through to the twenty-first century.

Is an executive information system an aid to good management?

Yes, but it is not a substitute for good management.

When should I start work on an executive information system?

Now, for it will take at least two years from the word go until the system starts to deliver really mature benefits.

Will the job then be finished?

No, for – as we have already said several times and make no apology for repeating – an executive information system is about changing management processes. And management processes should always evolve to meet new challenges.

And what can be gained from installing an executive information system?

The richest prize of all – the competitive edge that ensures future business success.

APPENDIX

Common executive information terms.

Alert: much shorter term for homeostatic report (qv).
Application: term for all the software and data needed to perform a particular task on the computer.
Architecture: the structure of the various components of a computer system, including hardware, software and communications, and how they fit together.
Business intelligence system: less used term for 'enterprise information system' (qv).
Context-sensitive help: on-screen information accessed to help resolve a difficulty in using an executive information system. The information that appears in the help screen should relate directly to the task you were performing when you called for the help.
Critical success factor: a feature of the company's operations or activities that is central to achieving its business mission and objectives. John Rockart, writing in the *Harvard Business Review*, calls critical success factors 'the limited number of areas in which results, if they are satisfactory, will ensure competitive performance for the organisation'.
Data provider: manager or organisation providing data for an executive information system. The data provider could be inside the organisation, such as a department or subsidiary, or outside the organisation, such as an on-line database like Reuters.
Data slice: information taken from a multi-dimensional database against given criteria. A two-dimensional data slice would show

information against two parameters (i.e. sales against time) a three-dimensional data slice against three parameters (i.e. sales by region against time).

Decision conferencing: the use of technology to help facilitate decision making in groups. The technology will typically help the participants to access the information they need and then analyse and prioritise it. The technology may also provide facilities for voting on possible decisions.

Decision support system: terms generally used to describe the family of systems immediately below an executive information system in a typical corporate hierarchical information pyramid. The systems help managers to retrieve and analyse data so that they can focus on specific data which helps them reach a decision.

Drill-down: the technique by which the user of an executive information system can gain access to the detailed components of a particular figure. Depending on the executive information system users can drill-down from one to several levels, with three or four being the most common number of levels.

Enterprise information system: a system sharing the same kinds of technologies as an executive information system, such as graphical user interfaces, easy to follow menus and an executive database, but designed for use by lower tiers of management.

Exception reporting: method of highlighting figures that do not conform to the expected (for example, that exceed or fall short of budget). Normally performed in an executive information system by showing the exceptions on screen in a different colour.

Executive champion: senior manager who drives the day-to-day work of building an executive information system, and who often reports to the executive sponsor.

Executive information system: computer system specifically designed with graphical user-friendly interfaces and easy-to-use features for senior executives. John Rockart and Michael Treacy in their paper 'The ceo goes on line' (*Harvard Business Review*) said that executive information systems share the following 'a central purpose; a common core data; two principle methods of use which are (1) access to the current status and projected trends of the business, and (2) personalised analyses of the available data; and a support organisation.'

Executive sponsor: a senior manager whose enthusiasm for a new executive information project provides the high-level guidance and promotion to help the project succeed.

Goal seeking: technique of using features in an executive information system to find out the steps that need to be taken to reach a given objective.

Groupware: term given to describe software that links together a team of people performing different roles on the same task. Although not synonymous with executive information systems, there can be strong groupware features in an executive information system when several managers are working together to take shared decisions and also access the same executive database.

Homeostatic report: an item of information about any subject that can threaten the business mission of the user company or department. Typically, the executive information system is programmed to display the information on-screen as soon as it arrives in the system, irrespective of whether the screen is being used for another purpose.

Hot spot: a coloured on-screen button that has been preprogrammed to enable an executive information system user to perform a particular task.

Hybrid manager: term given to a manager who combines technical knowledge of information technology with a sound business understanding of the areas in which the technology needs to be applied.

Key performance indicator: a measurement devised to determine whether a critical success factor is being achieved. There can be more than one key performance indicator for each critical success factor.

Knowledge-based system: computer containing a body of specialised knowledge and a set of pre-programmed inferences which help the user to understand and take decisions in the subject area.

Mouse: small pushable desk-top device with a roller wheel underneath which moves cursor on screen. Buttons on the mouse (usually one or two) are clicked in order to activate on-screen instructions.

Multi-dimensional database: software which holds facts and figures in a way that enables them to be accessed in a variety of different ways by such parameters as time, operating unit, product line, salesperson, etc.

Multimedia: combination of text, graphs, pictures, video, sound and voice in an application delivered through a PC or workstation.

Prototyping: technique of developing an application step by step so that the user's comments and suggestions can be incorporated in the next stage of the development.

Real-time: ability to obtain constantly updated information from a computer without delay.

Touch screen: special computer screen programmed so that actions take place when user touches an on-screen command.

Traffic lighting: way of showing figures on screen in order to denote their status i.e. green = on budget; orange = slightly adrift from budget; red = seriously adrift from budget.

Variance reporting: technique which allows the user to instruct the executive information system to traffic light any figure which deviates by more than a given amount or percentage from the norm or budget.

REFERENCES

Chapter 1

1. Galbraith, John Kenneth, *The New Industrial Estate*, Houghton Mifflin (1967)
2. Henley Centre for Forecasting, *Tomorrow's Business Priorities* (1991)
3. Harvey-Jones, John, *Making It Happen*, Collins (1988)
4. Iacocca, Lee, *Iacocca: an autobiography*, Sidgwick and Jackson (1985)
5. Mintzberg, Henry, *The Nature of Managerial Work*, Harper & Row, NY (1973)
6. Slocum, John W., and Hellriegel, Don, *How Managers' Minds Work* cited by Irwin P. Jarrett, 'Improving Financial Reporting', conference presentation (1990).
7. Isenberg, Daniel, 'How Senior Managers Think', *Harvard Business Review* (Nov-Dec 1984)

Chapter 2

1. KPMG Peat Marwick Management Consultants, *Information for Strategic Management* (1990)
2. Handy, Charles, *Understanding Organisations*, 3rd edition, Penguin Business Library (1985)
3. Gibson, C. and Bund-Jackson, B., *The Information Imperative*, Lexington Books, US
4. Rockart, John, and De Long, David, *Executive Support Systems for Top Management Computer Use*, Dow Jones-Irwin (1988)

Chapter 3

1. Strassmann, Paul, *The Business Value of Computers*, Collier (1991)
2. Goodman, Danny, *The Hypercard Handbook*, Apple Computer
3. Business Intelligence: *The EIS Market in the UK and Europe*, (1990)
4. Develin & Partners, *Tackling the IT development backlog* (1991)
5. Austin, Noel, 'A management support environment', *ICL Technical Journal* (Nov 1986)

Chapter 4

1. British Computer Society, *From potential to reality*, (1990)
2. Business Intelligence Executive Forum: *Key Factors in Developing an EIS* (1990)
3. Business Intelligence: *The EIS Market in the UK and Europe* (1990)
4. Business Intelligence, *EIS: a study of costs and benefits*, 2nd edition (1991)

Chapter 5

1. Rockart, John, 'Chief executives define their own data needs', *Harvard Business Review* (Mar-Apr 1979)
2. Keynes, John Maynard, *General Theory of Employment*
3. De Long, David, 'Leaders and Laggers in EIS: the US Experience', conference presentation (1991)
4. King, Peter, 'Managing Data Quality', conference presentation (1989)
5. Thomas, David, 'A Framework for EIS Planning and Project Management', conference presentation (1989)

Chapter 7

1. Bittlestone, Robert, *Executive Information for Strategic Control*, Metapraxis (1991)

Chapter 8

1. Handy, Charles, *Sticking to your knitting, View '90 – the synchronised business*, Andersen Consulting (1990)
2. Nolan Norton Institute, *Executive Strategy*, Autumn 1991
3. Peters, Tom, *Thriving on chaos*, Pan Books (1989)

INDEX

Aer Rianta,
  example, 48
AIU UK,
  example, 29
Andersen Consulting, 97
Austin, Noel, 48

Babcock Energy,
  example, 77
Bittlestone, Robert, 127
Boots the Chemist,
  example, 75
BP Chemicals,
  example, 81
Briefing books, 30, 105, 125
Brent Walker Group,
  example, 43
British Airways, 2, 36, 65
  example, 76, 120
British Computer Society, 58
British Rail Network Southeast,
  example, 76
British Steel Distribution,
  example, 84, 125
BT,
  example, 71
Bund-Jackson, B., 35
Business strategy, 45

Cellular technology, 141
Champions, 58, 61–64
Charts, 107–9
Chief executives, 52, 119
  applications, 121
CIBA Geigy UK,
  example, 122
Cooperative processing, 37
Cooperative Wholesale Society,
  example, 53
Corporate structure, 44
Critical success factors, 82–3, 136
  features, 84
Courage Take Home Trade,
  example, 123
Customer service, 44, 116

Data, 59
  adding value, 94
Data-driven reporting, 9
Data ownership, 89
Data provider, 58
Data slices, 107
Decision making, 36, 43
Decision support system, 38
De Long, David, 35, 89, 90, 93
Develin & Partners, 46
Disraeli, Benjamin, 134

151

Divisional executives, 124
Drill down, 9, 43, 106

Eastern Electricity, 131
Economic changes, 14
Enterprise Miniere et Chemique,
  example, 42
Executive information systems,
  adding value, 96
  application areas, 127
  budget, 60
  business issues, 58
  business processes, 75
  choice, 55–78
  communications, 77
  cooperative processing, 66
  core data, 4
  cost savings, 74
  development method, 60
  executive database, 7
  data collection and
    consolidation, 8
  definition, 2
  development tools, 10
  first application, 79–87
  first generation, 37
  history, 35–8
  implementation, 79–101
  interfaces, 6
  investigational techniques, 9
  issues to consider, 54
  IT strategy, 46
  justification, 72–8
  local area network, 66
  main components, 6–10
  mainframe computers, 65
  managing change, 134
  mid-range system, 65
  necessary features, 32
  organisation impact, 114–17
  PC, 65, 68
  planning techniques, 9
  politics, 58, 87–90
  problem solving, 40–45, 75
  project manager, 58

purpose, 4
reasons for wanting one, 46
reporting, 74
second generation, 37
selection criteria, 70
shareholder value analysis, 138
support organisation, 5
third generation, 37
time saving, 76
troublemakers, 57
two methods of use, 4
use, 103–17
users, 51
when needed, 39–54
Executive information systems
    applications,
  cash flow, 137
  global control, 137
  goal seeking, 137
  market place performance, 138
  performance-based
    compensation, 138
  total quality management, 137
Executive work, 19–23
Executives,
  information needs, 26–35
  roles, 20
Expert systems, 139
External data, 41

Fast Moving Consumer Goods,
  applications, 128
Financial directors, 52
Financial executives, 121
  applications, 123
Financial reporting, 42
Financial services,
  applications, 129

Galbraith, John Kenneth, 11
Gateway Foodmarkets,
  example, 53
Gibson, C., 35
Goodman, Danny, 42

Goold, Michael, 27
GPT, 128
Graphs, 107

Handy, Charles, 35, 133
Harvard Business Review, 3
Help screens, 109
Hybrid managers, 58
Hellriegel, Don, 21
Henley Centre for Forecasting, 17
Hierarchies,
  changing structure, 17

IBM,
  example, 17
ICI,
  example, 99, 120
ICI Paints,
  example, 41
Information,
  business input, 11–13
  overload, 16
Infra-red keypad, 105
Investigational techniques, 107
Isenberg, Daniel, 22
IT architecture, 48

Key performance indicators, 82–3
Keyboard, 105
Keynes, John Maynard, 11, 87
King, Peter, 93
KPMG Management Consultants,
  27

Laptop computers, 141
Laser printers, 141
London Underground,
  example, 75

Management information system,
  38
Management productivity, 41
Management support
  professionals, 125
  applications, 126

Managing directors – see chief
  executives,
Manufacturing,
  applications, 128
Marketing executives, 53, 123
  applications, 124
Mental model, 23, 31, 40
Microsoft, 140
Minster Insurance,
  example, 18
Mintzberg, Henry, 20, 35
MK Electric, 128
Modelling, 9, 35, 117
Mouse, 105
Mulroy, June,
  example, 21
Multimedia, 141

Naisbitt, John, 18
Nolan Norton Institute, 136

Object-oriented programs, 140
OKI Europe,
  example, 77
Oxford Institute of Information
  Management, 55

Peters, Tom, 136
Phantom fighter,
  example, 13
Phillips Petroleum, 2
Post Office Corporation,
  example, 120
Powszechny Bank Gospodarezy,
  example, 45
Prototyping, 91–3
Public authorities,
  applications, 132

Quinn, John, J., 27

RAF Strike Command, 132
Rank Xerox,
  example, 52
Reck, Robert, 20

Retailing,
  applications, 130
Rockart, John, 3, 35, 82
Royal Insurance, 130
Royal Mail,
  example, 44

Sales executives, 123
  application, 124
Simon Engineering,
  example, 122
Single European Market, 14
Slocum, John, W., 21
South Lincolnshire Health
  Authority, 132
Span of control, 116
Sponsors, 58, 61–4
Stephenson, George, 2
Strassmann, Paul 41
Structured interviewing, 85
Subsidiary executives, 124
  applications, 125
Sun Microsystems,
  example, 74

Texas Homecare,
  example, 44

Thomas, David, 97
Thorn EMI,
  example, 120
Toshiba UK,
  example, 40
Touch screen, 105
Training, 103–4
Transport Development Group,
  115
Treacy, Michael, 3

UB Brands, 129
Utilities,
  application, 131

Wallace, Robert, 2
Wessex Water, 131
  example, 45
Windows, 140
Woolwich Building Society, 130

Xerox Corporation,
  example, 135

Yorkshire Building Society,
  example, 85